ALSO BY SLOANE CROSLEY

I Was Told There'd Be Cake

essays

How Did You

Get This Number

Sloane Crosley

RIVERHEAD BOOKS

New York

RIVERHEAD BOOKS
Published by the Penguin Group
Penguin Group (USA) Inc.
375 Hudson Street, New York, New York 10014, USA
Penguin Group (Canada), 90 Eglinton Avenue East, Suite 700, Toronto, Ontario M4P 2Y3, Canada
(a division of Pearson Penguin Canada Inc.)
Penguin Books Ltd., 80 Strand, London WC2R 0RL, England
Penguin Group Ireland, 25 St. Stephen's Green, Dublin 2, Ireland (a division of Penguin Books Ltd.)
Penguin Group (Australia), 250 Camberwell Road, Camberwell, Victoria 3124, Australia
(a division of Pearson Australia Group Pty. Ltd.)
Penguin Books India Pvt. Ltd., 11 Community Centre, Panchsheel Park, New Delhi—110 017, India
Penguin Group (NZ), 67 Apollo Drive, Rosedale, Auckland 0632, New Zealand
(a division of Pearson New Zealand Ltd.)
Penguin Books (South Africa) (Pty.) Ltd., 24 Sturdee Avenue, Rosebank, Johannesburg 2196,
South Africa

Penguin Books Ltd., Registered Offices: 80 Strand, London WC2R 0RL, England

In the interest of privacy, names and identifying characteristics have been changed, timelines have been compressed, and some of the dialogue is more exact than some of the other dialogue. Although subject to impression and memory, this is a work of nonfiction. The events described have happened. Except, of course, for a couple of passages, which I'm pretty sure have been so distorted by interpretation that no place and no one involved with them actually exist, including myself, including you.

The following stories have appeared, in somewhat different form, in the following publications:
"Lost in Space" in Salon; "Light Pollution" in Vice.

Copyright © 2010 by Sloane Crosley
Book design by Meighan Cavanaugh

First Riverhead hardcover edition: June 2010
First Riverhead trade paperback edition: May 2011

Riverhead trade paperback ISBN: 978-1-59448-519-0

The Library of Congress has catalogued the Riverhead hardcover edition as follows:

Crosley, Sloane.
How did you get this number: essays / Sloane Crosley.
  p.   cm.
ISBN 978-1-59448-759-0
I. Title.
PS3603 R673H69   2010   2010007178
814'.6—dc22

PRINTED IN THE UNITED STATES OF AMERICA

10   9   8   7   6   5   4   3   2   1

*Penguin is committed to publishing works of quality and integrity.
In that spirit, we are proud to offer this book to our readers;
However, the story, the experiences, and the words
are the author's alone.*

To my parents. For everything.*

---

* Everything except the two-week period in 1995 directly following the time you went to Ohio for a wedding and I threw a party in the house, which is the most normal thing a teenage American can do, aside from lie about it, which I also did, and Mom eyed me suspiciously for days, morphing into a one-woman Scotland Yard, marching into my bedroom with a fistful of lint from the dryer to demonstrate that I had mysteriously washed all the towels, and then she waited until we were in a nice restaurant to scream, "Someone vomited on my couch, I know it!" and Dad took away my automotive privileges straight through college so that I spent the subsequent four years likening you both to Stasi foot soldiers, confined as I was to a campus-on-the-hill when I could have been learning how to play poker at the casinos down the road and making bad decisions at townie bars. I think we can all agree you overreacted.

For everything except that, I am profoundly grateful. I have only the greatest affection for you now. Also: I vomited on the couch.

He had no especial desire to meet or to know any of these people; all he demanded was the right to look on and conjecture, to watch the pageant. . . . He was now entirely rid of his nervous misgivings, of his forced aggressiveness, of the imperative desire to show himself different from his surroundings. He felt now that his surroundings explained him. Nobody questioned the purple; he had only to wear it passively. He had only to glance down at his attire to reassure himself that here it would be impossible for anyone to humiliate him.

—WILLA CATHER, "PAUL'S CASE," 1905

CONTENTS

Show Me on the Doll

There is only one answer to the question: Would you like to see a three a.m. performance of amateur Portuguese circus clowns?

But as I sat in an open-air bar on my last night in Lisbon, drinking wine with my coat still on, I couldn't bring myself to give it. These weren't the universally frightening species of clown, the ones who are never not scary. No one likes a clown who reminds them of why they hate ice-cream-truck music. These were more the Cirque du Soleil–type clown. The attractive jesters found on the backs of playing cards. They had class. They had top hats. And I? I had a pocketful of change I couldn't count. I had paid for my wine in the dark by opening my hand and allowing the bartender to remove the correct coins, as if he were delousing my palm. It was the December before I turned thirty. I was in a place I had no business being. The last thing

I needed was a front-row seat to some carnie hipster adaptation of *Eyes Wide Shut*.

Besides, I had nothing left to prove. When you spin a globe and point to a city and actually go to that city, you build an allowance of missed opportunities on the back end. No one could accuse me of not living in the moment if I opted out of one lousy underground freak show. I had done enough on the risk-taking front just by it being winter and me being the sole American in all of Lisbon. If you had taken a flash census of the city, you might have found a few other Americans, businessmen and women holed up in three-star hotel suites, surrounded by a variety of ineffective lighting options. But I knew in the pit of my stomach that I was the only tourist from my country drifting around Europe's sea capital.

While the emotional sum total of my trip would eventually add up to happiness, while I would feel a protective bond with the few objects I acquired in Lisbon—a necklace from a street fair, a piece of cracked tile, a pack of Portuguese cigarettes called "Portuguese"—hidden between the cathedral and castle tours was the truth: I have never felt more alone than I did in Lisbon. A human being can spend only so much time outside her comfort zone before she realizes she is still tethered to it. Like a dog on one of those retractable leashes, I had made it all the way to Europe's curb when I began to feel a slight tug around my neck.

The problem wasn't merely the total annihilation of English, as if English had taken too many sets of X-rays at the dentist's office and had been radiated to the point of disintegration. I do not roam the planet assuming that everyone speaks English. The problem was I dove headlong into an off-season culture that assumes everyone speaks Portuguese. A delusion that I adopted at first, and that inspired a temporary Portuguese patriotism in me, accompanied by a self-shaming for not being fluent myself. I had traveled to Romance-language regions before, sometimes alone, and found that as much as people like you to attempt communication in their language, what they like even more is for you to stop butchering it. In most cultures, the natives will let you get about four sentences in before they put you out of your misery. In Portugal, I kept waiting for that kindly metaphorical hand to reach across the pastry counter or the gift-shop register, pinch my tongue, and say, "Enough already." I was going to be waiting a long time. How poorly did I have to imitate their infamously irregular verbs before someone squished my cheeks into submission? Was this place not "sleepy," as the guidebooks described, but completely unconscious?

In the time I spent there, I barely heard Spanish or German or Russian, either. My ears captured the clunky tones of English but once—and from an elderly British couple seated behind me on a wooden tram. With a controlled panic in their voices, they discussed the winding route of the tram and the seemingly arbitrary stops. It was a conversation that might not have caused a fight had it taken place on still ground. But their words were becoming heated as the wife's devil-may-care attitude clashed with her husband's conviction that they were being whisked away from the city's center into sketchier pastures. The tiff ended with the husband making his wife unbutton her coat, sling her purse over her shoulder, and put her coat back on over that.

"Just do it, Joan," he said through his teeth. "Don't make a scene about it."

Joan complied, temporarily pacifying her husband. This new costume made her look like one of the ancient Portuguese ladies, their spines bobbing beneath their cardigans as they scaled the city's steep inclines. The jostling act of transformation, of removing arms from sleeves and slinging bags on shoulders, also made her a more obvious bait for pickpockets. In the end she resembled a cartoon of a boa constrictor that had just swallowed a lawn chair. The resulting image is not one of a pregnant snake but of a snake who has just swallowed a lawn chair.

I considered saying something, engaging with them. I was relieved by the sound of kindred vowels. Days of talking exclusively to myself and I was finally ready to take the gag out of my throat and rejoin the land of fluency. Lack of human-on-human communication works like a liquid fast— first you miss the solid sustenance, then for a long time you wonder why you ever needed it, then you miss it so acutely it makes you dizzy. I assumed a symbiotic need for these Brits to break their fast. I could be their conversational prune juice. But when they made their way to my end of the tram in preparation for the next stop, I just stared at them with the passive contempt of a local.

I FOUND MYSELF WAITING ON LINE FOR LISBON'S main attraction: an antique freestanding elevator that springs up the city's center and leads to nowhere. When I got to the highest level, I climbed the narrowest staircase to the tippy top. *America is lacking in this,* I thought. All of our public structures are self-explanatory. When you press the PH button, you're going to the penthouse. Not the stairs that lead to the landing that lead to the lookout above the penthouse. Our basements are conveniently located at the base. No cellars that lead to subfloors that lead to catacombs of ruins. *The Goonies* was just that one time, and it was a movie.

The wind blew hard as I leaned on a railing that would have been ripe for a lawsuit if this was Paris's Eiffel Tower or Seattle's Space Needle. My calves throbbed from days of rushing through Lisbon's seven hills as if I had anywhere to go. I was like a cat that urgently needs to be on the other side of the room for no apparent reason. I looked out toward the ocean in the direction of home, squinting at the horizon.

Then I apologized to the travel gods for thinking I could do this, remembering there's a reason we don't always fulfill the wishes of our younger selves once we're grown.

The idea of going to Lisbon began as a bastard idea, the daughter of impulse and video montages with a drop of *Casablanca* in there somewhere. On occasion, it occurs to adults that they are allowed to do all the things that being a child prevented them from doing. But those desires change while you're not looking. There was a time when your favorite color transferred from purple to blue to whatever shade it is when you realize having a favorite color is a trite personality crutch, an unsubtle cultivation of quirk and a possible cry for help. You just don't notice the time line of your own metamorphosis. Until you do. Every once in a while, time dissolves and you remember what you liked as a kid. You jump on your hotel bed, order dessert first, decide to put every piece of jewelry you own on your body and leave the house. Why? Because you can. Because you're the boss. Because . . . *Ooooh. Shiny.*

One day in November, I came home and saw the desk globe on my bookshelf. Instead of seeing it as my globe in my apartment, where I come home every day, I remembered the globe I had when I was twelve years old. And saw it as a challenge. Confined by perfectly manicured lawns and freshly tarred driveways, preteen me had promised myself that one day I would spin and point and travel wherever my finger landed. I loved the movie *Better Off Dead*, that self-hating love letter from suburban America to foreign exchange students everywhere. More than just a snow-snorting lesson in obsession, here was a cautionary tale against armchair traveling. A rallying call to leaving one's immediate area code immediately. If I didn't get a passport soon, I might grow up and find myself serving French fries and French dressing to visiting Parisians.

With each passing year, the promise would become harder to keep. I was about to turn thirty. The obligations, they were coming. What they would entail, I couldn't say, but I sensed they would be obligatory. So I made some rules:

1. No traveling to places that would deplete my life savings getting there.
2. No war zones.
3. No places I had been before.

And finally:

4. No places so romantic they would depress the foie gras out of me.

I closed my eyes and pushed. I was prepared to go to South America or South Dakota. I was prepared to go to Iceland in the middle of winter or to Ulaanbaatar in the middle of Mongolia. Contingent on fare restrictions and blackout dates for Ulaanbaatar Air. I stuck my finger on the spinning world to make it stop.

It landed at the corner of 20°N and the Tropic of Cancer, smack in the center of the Pacific. For the briefest of moments, I saw myself floating on a raft, gazing at the stars, using coconut shells for a bra. . . . This wasn't so bad. Then I imagined becoming a member of that select club of people in human history who have resorted to drinking their own urine. New rule:

5. No ocean.

When I spun again, I touched down on Lisbon. Either my globe is especially small or my fingertip especially fat, but you could argue I was also pointing to Morocco. I made a face. Should a woman really be traveling to Morocco by herself right now? Exactly how dedicated was I to this pact business? Reality was pounding with both fists. A few more sensible thought cycles and I wouldn't be going anywhere.

So I booked a flight to Lisbon, set to depart in one week.

Here's a travel tip: If you're booking an international flight for no particular reason to a relatively obscure city and do not plan on buying or selling drugs when you get there, try to make your reservations at least two weeks beforehand. Otherwise, your boarding pass will be marked with a secret code suggesting you are, in fact, a potential drug or arms vendor, and you will be taken to a special room and treated as such by airport security. Take it or leave it.

The twelve-year-old in me was thrilled by adventuring, picturing an animation of my plane hovering over a map of the Atlantic, heading east, a charming single-engine sound coming incongruously from the 747. Back in real time, I packed my things, hailed a cab, sat in traffic, looked out the window, and wondered what the hell I was doing. Then I sat at the gate with a bunch of Portuguese people who also wondered what the hell I was doing. People carry themselves differently when they have a reason to move from point A to point B. Waiting on line for the bathroom somewhere over the Atlantic, I could feel a teenage girl burrowing a hole in the back of my head with her eyes. When I turned to meet her stare, she asked me if I was Portuguese.

"No, I'm not." I smiled and turned back around. She tapped me on the shoulder and held her fingers together. She squinted through the space in between to indicate "a little." That, or she was crushing my head.

"None."

She tapped again.

"Porquê Portugal?"

She was probably being held captive on a family vacation and couldn't understand why a free woman such as myself would go voluntarily to prison when I could be eating dessert first and jumping on hotel beds. It's how I still feel about

Williamsburg, Virginia. But days later, as I stood at the top of an ornamental elevator with breathtaking three-hundred-sixty-degree views of Lisbon, I recalled her incredulous attitude. I struggled both to breathe into the wind and to remember why I had come here. In one of the last scenes of *Breakfast at Tiffany's*, Audrey Hepburn is preparing to leave for Brazil by listening to Portuguese on tape.

"I believe you are in league with the butcher," she says, proudly declaring the English translation of what she has heard.

"I believe you are in league with the butcher," I said to the air. And the air blew my words back in my face.

I gripped a rusted railing and walked down to a small café, where a three-person band played fado music for the tourists. Except there were no tourists at the café. Just a handful of Portuguese families. They looked unhappy, with their elbows holding down paper tablecloths and their jackets zipped to their chins. It had been six days. I hadn't communicated with anyone here or at home since I landed. I had nowhere to go. I bought an orange soda and gulped it down. Here was another thing you'd never find in America: glass bottles distributed on fence-free, poorly manned thirty-story towers. What a trusting and carefree people the Portuguese were! Even if I couldn't understand a single word they said. I tried to remember what it was that Holly Golightly had translated. Perhaps if I could pluck out "In you I believe" I could strike up a very earnest conversation with someone.

LIKE EVERY TWENTY-NINE-YEAR-OLD WITH A DATE of birth and a driver's license, I had spent the past year being asked if I was "freaking out" about turning thirty. I took pride in my blasé response. What was there to freak out about? One day I'd be fifty and both shamed by and envious of my dread of thirty. Besides, a new decade is a chance to find oneself at the beginning of things. Oh, life. What a sweet little Etch A Sketch of time you are! Only now, in Lisbon's central square, watching a one-eyed man play the accordion while surrounded by stray Chihuahuas, did it occur to me that just maybe *this* was the freak-out. I swore that if I had to do it over again, I'd exorcise my panic attack like a normal person—by getting sloppy drunk. And I wouldn't do it in euros. I swore that I wasn't too cool to grip the ankles of the next nice couple I saw and beg them to take me with them, wherever they were going.

Instead of doing that, I decided to make the best of it and hunt down an eighteenth-century opera house. This took me half a day.

On top of the language barrier, I had the labyrinth of Bairro Alto with which to contend. Perhaps the oldest part of the city was not the wisest destination for someone with no sense of direction. It is impossible to overstate the percentage of time I spent lost in Lisbon. There are large swaths of the city for which there are no maps. You can't buy them, they don't exist, stop asking. Some streets simply don't have names. At one point I found myself spat out onto a relatively trafficked road and played the classic game of mime-slash-baseball-catcher with a well-meaning Portuguese woman. She studied my foldout map. I studied her studying the map. Her eyes bounced from squiggle to squiggle in curious panic. Wanting to pitch in, I attempted to speak Portuguese by severely mumbling Spanish. Which I also don't speak.

When people regale one another with embarrassing foibles, one person will often claim that another looked at them "as if they were retarded." This woman's face is what they are referring to.

After some time she discerned where I wanted to go, and I discerned that she used to live in this very neighborhood. What luck! We parted ways. Half an hour later, when I finally located the street, it was just lying there—exactly one block parallel from where I first received my directions. What would I do if I had a Portuguese pen pal? I imagined trying to address the envelope. Wedged between the person's name and the city I might put: *Two lefts and a right but more of an uphill right, then make another left and go up the stairs until you hit a nine-pronged fork in the road. Take the street that's the second from your right and look for the house with the light blue shutters. Not the baby blue shutters. If you've hit the men hot-wiring a Vespa, you've gone too far.*

Thus I found myself meandering down a pedestrian-less

street I had just been down ten minutes prior, tipped off by the specific network of clotheslines and the mismatched garments that hung from them. When I turned around again, I saw a figure of a man approaching. He wore a silver windbreaker that glimmered cheesily in the daylight. Since I placed no stock in one direction over the other, I decided to continue walking away from the man. But each time I turned an Escheresque corner, he turned the same corner. I was torn between behaving like the paranoid Brits on the tram and imitating the street sense of a native Lisboan. I could hear him getting closer. The guidebooks and hotel staff alike had warned me about pickpockets (the former in complete sentences, the latter via an unsolicited staging of the crime using a sucking candy and my personal space). But would a pickpocket really chase me down an alley? Is that not like a cat burglar with Tourette's? Or a eunuch rapist? *With what?* The question is begged. Some people don't have the physical skill set for a life of crime.

This not-so-private detective began cooing to me as if I were an underloved house pet—he had no real passion for catching me but felt obliged to go through the motions. Still, the distance between us was closing. Somewhere above, a kitchen window was open. I heard lunch being prepared and a sporting match on the radio. I could hear the plays of the game, so absent was any foot traffic on the street. I got the distinct feeling that people were attacked on this little bend of cobblestone all the time. Probably they were victims of petty crime or sexual harassment or found their faces on the business end of a broken bottle. And this probably wasn't a good thing. But it probably wasn't that big a deal, either.

In all fairness, it should be said that Lisbon is hardly a shady place. Twenty years ago, fresh out of the womb of fascism, it was. And one can still witness hints of this on the outskirts of the city, in the condition of the churches built in 1980, which are often so badly battered that they're indiscernible from those built in 1680. The past is in plain sight in the form of ashtrays on public buses and spray-painted swastikas on the sides of apartment towers. But Lisbon is also a delicate place that's been sucked into the modern world quickly. There are major international design fairs and direct flights that come here now. My most posh English friend spent her summers here and unironically encouraged me to visit a bar called Snob. Lisbon's biggest nightclub is owned by John Malkovich.

I was not afraid of John Malkovich. I was not even afraid of getting mugged in Bushwick. Okay, Greenpoint. I was not even afraid of getting mugged in Greenpoint. So, what then? Was this real fear or just some manifestation of acute loneliness, the kind that afflicts people abandoned on desert islands or raised by wolves? Though even victims of first contact are probably less seized by terror than I was. Honestly, if you thought you had the only

pineapple in the world and I came to your house and gave
you a second pineapple, how long would it take you to get
over the shock? Not very long. The real reason island dwell-
ers and jungle orphans try to shoot you with poison darts
before they meet you is that they instinctually mistrust their
own kind.

By this time I had made a few more turns. I could hear
footsteps descending the worn marble staircase behind me.
That's when I came upon a set of poultry. Two portly chick-
ens blocked my path, brains too small to focus on their feet.
Behind me, the footsteps reached the bottom of the stairs.
All I had to do was keep walking. A few more turns and
I'd be safe—either out of the labyrinth or hidden farther
within it. For reasons still not fully known to me I stopped.
I searched my jacket pockets, feeling for my camera. Maybe
I wanted proof that I had been here so that when my body
was found in the Tejo River, my camera still on my person,
the police would have clues. Maybe I wanted to tempt fate or
to make some larger sharklike point that once I stopped running, he would stop chasing me. Maybe I just liked the artis-
tic composition of land fowl. I saw a flash of silver catching
up with me.

"Shit," I muttered.

"Hola, gata!" He raised his voice. "Where you going?"

I had no idea. Oh, how you cut to the core of me, random Portuguese thief! I quickly snapped a picture of the
chickens.

He was close enough for me to hear the swoosh of his pants as he approached. *Jesus,* I thought, *is he wearing a full-body tracksuit? What is that, nylon?* The chickens straightened their necks in his direction. They looked frightened and stupid. I clutched my camera in my hand and quickly speed-walked back to civilization.

SNOB WAS A PLACE WHERE I SAT AT A FELT-TOP table illuminated by a desk lamp. I watched soccer with a few senior citizens. They were as surprised by my presence as I was unsurprised by theirs. Apparently, the whole scene becomes just that—a scene. It transforms into a chic hotspot sometime around two a.m. I could see how, when filled up a bit more, the bar might not have been the most depressing watering hole of its generation. I glanced at my watch. Eleven p.m. The foray into an advanced time zone was working in my favor, but the language barrier was not. I was caught in socialization purgatory. If I left Snob, the situation elsewhere would be just as dead, lonely, reminiscent of game night at Jean-Paul Sartre's house, etc. But if I waited for things to heat up, I'd be equally overwhelmed. Lisbon is designed for bar crawls and multilevel discos that close after sunrise, for nights that make your top-ten lists: Top Ten Drunkest. Top Ten Wildest. Top Ten Involving Grain Alcohol, a Leotard, and a Spider Monkey. I wish someone had told me this. But how could anyone have? How could anyone have warned me that a Saturday night in Lisbon rivals Ibiza in dry-ice expenditures? I never asked.

One of the old men tore himself away from the game to bring me a bar menu. I ordered a basket of fried pierogi filled with shrimp and cream cheese. I took one bite and stared at the TV for two more matches. Has anyone in history been more engrossed in a televised sporting event? I drank two whiskey sodas and got into a cab. Because the roads of central Lisbon cut in and out of each other at such windy angles, the bad news is that it took me a few minutes to realize my driver was drunk. The good news is that there is such a thing as the international language of slurring. As soon as I had a bead on the neighborhood of my hotel, I asked him to let me out. Elaborate Christmas-light formations were strung above the roads. My head spun. I walked up to my hotel, grateful to have made it home. Even if I was greeted by a broken radiator and a lone bath towel that could tear the skin off a baby.

I turned on the radio and listened to the news in Portuguese, which was delivered with such enthusiasm that it was impossible to separate from the commercials that buffered it. I sat on my rock-hard bed and, not finding a remote, got back up to turn on the TV. There are ten zillion channels in Portugal. Half of them are QVC. Almost half of them are porn. And everything in between is both. I can't tell you how many late-night programs I stumbled upon in which a topless woman in a Santa hat bounced up and down behind a counter of state-of-the-art blenders. Or how many men with Burt Reynolds mustaches came up behind these women brandishing sex toys that, upon closer inspection, were meant to peel carrots. Have you ever seen a naked woman jerk off a paper-cup dispenser? Have you? Some things can't be unseen.

I clicked off the bedside lamp and went to bed, pulling the covers above my head. Streaming in through the rough lace of the bedspread were splotches of the light from the apartments and restaurants up the hill. I could hear glasses clinking, people laughing on balconies, lovers fighting in the streets. This was, hands down, the most pathetic day of my twenties.

————

BUT THE NEXT MORNING, THE BEGINNING OF MY
last day in Lisbon, something had changed. I woke up at a
reasonable hour. I stretched and cranked open my window
and stood at the far corner, where I could see the fog rolling over the river and the two perfect peaks of the bridge
sticking up through it. Down the hill, the city was a mix of
browns and reds and stucco. Seagulls flew over the palm
trees along the shore, palm trees that I had failed to notice
before. *It's going to be a good day,* I thought. I turned on the
TV to see one of Santa's elf slaves, still naked and still riding a vacuum cleaner. She shook her breasts in agreement.
A good day indeed.

In the military, they have a kind of sanctioned hazing so
systemic that even the recipients get on board. They break you
down so they can build you back up again, a friend once told
me. And perhaps that's what Lisbon had done to me—made
me feel lost and stupid and envious of those who don't feel lost
and stupid. Only so I could begin the next day feeling profoundly lucky to be there. The city and I had been in the shit
together, fused into a state of understanding, despite our differ-
ences. I looked in my guidebook and memorized "good morning" in Portuguese, repeating it aloud like a phone number
fresh from the operator: *Bom dia. Bom dia. Bom dia, como vai?*

I walked down to the river and miraculously found my

way back to the hotel without asking for directions. The winds of luck were no longer blowing straight into my face. It was as if I was reborn with a traveling superpower. The power to discern. Here is what to order for breakfast today. Here are the right buttons to press on the ticket machine. Here is the bus you want. There is a sweet teenage boy, and behind him is the sweet teenage boy who will steal all your money. I went east, to Belém, a neighborhood known for its elaborate monastery and custard tarts. I went to the monastery, where I sat down and thought generally of God. With its interior of candelabras and stained glass and exterior of endless spires dripping with concrete saints, it made American churches look like Fisher-Price models of Christ's house. It had the chaotic façade of the Sagrada Familia and the excessive buttress count of Notre Dame. I meandered through the manicured sculpture gardens, licking custard from my thumb. If I had only one pudding-like substance to consume for the rest of my life, it would be that custard.

When I reached the port, I discovered a monument jutting out over the water. *The Tribute to Explorers*, said the statue's stone name tag. The wind blew but seemed less adamant about choking me than it had been at the top of the freestanding elevator. I was standing on the exact piece of land where Christopher Columbus docked in 1493, when he returned from the Americas. A few years later, Vasco da Gama pushed off from the same spot.

I removed my shoes and dangled my legs over the stone cliff. I felt like a little kid at the dinner table, my feet bobbing in the air. I also felt connected to the people who inspired these statues. Subtract the scurvy, the smallpox, and the genocide infliction, and how different were we? I was comforted, thinking that not only had this trip to Lisbon been no accident, but also that these men had the same view of this river that I had now. Take away a building here and a bridge there, and how much could the curve of salt water have altered over the centuries? I looked up at the giant stone nostrils as they jutted out, permanently distracted by the scenery. The sun was setting on the horizon. The tarts were beginning to settle in my stomach. As I got up, I knocked one of my balled-up socks, which went tumbling down the stone and into the water below. Yesterday, this incident would have been tacked on to a chain of poorly executed attempts at tourism. But because this was today, I thought, *At least it wasn't the shoe.*

That night I found myself with a lower-than-usual tolerance for QVC porn. I paced in my room, making U's along the foot of the bed. On the nightstand my camera was running low on batteries. There were piles of brochures and keepsakes, napkins and matchbooks. Who knew they would be treated so preciously when they left their respective assembly lines? This was my last night here. I grabbed my coat. As I passed the man behind the front desk, I winked at him, punching my fists into my pockets and holding them close to my body so as to indicate an awareness of potential pickpockets.

I clomped down the uneven cobblestone hills. At the base of one staircase I could see electric lanterns framing the doorway of a café I had passed before. I hadn't gone in because I knew the staff had seen me from the windows, looking overwhelmed and guidebook-dependent each morning. I walked into what I expected to be a closet, but it turned out to be a sprawling, multi-balconied bar. At night, the café traded cappuccino for hard liquor. The back porch overlooked the bridge, the river, the castles and cathedrals—the whole city. I took out a paperback book, lifted my glass of wine from the bar, and settled on the balcony, where it was getting cold enough to see my own breath.

And then they sent in the clowns. A girl in her early twenties came into the bar and sat facing me a few tables away. After we exchanged the international head nod for

"You're at the same place as I am," she got up and sat one table closer.

"*Como vai?*" she said in Portuguese, followed by an "English?" in English.

She had thin blond hair with fuchsia streaks that crept out from beneath a propellerless beanie. Her eyeliner made me question the clarity of the mirrors in her house. Her right arm was covered with what looked like kabbalah bracelets. I wanted to tell her that I was fairly certain that karma points were not doled out in proportion to the number of bracelets you wore. But since I could barely ask for the cheese plate, I just smiled wider instead. *Si, English.*

She moved closer and sat next to me. I shut my book and smiled. I couldn't stop smiling. Not because I was thrilled at the prospect of hair and makeup tips from this woman but because it was my only means of expressing myself. I am not a professionally trained mime. My companion, on the other hand, probably was. She was wearing white gloves that stopped at her wrists. With them, she gestured at her two friends, who had just arrived at the bar. When that didn't work, she screeched at them in high-speed Portuguese. *She must do her training at remedial mime college,* I thought.

A boy and a girl, not older than twenty, came over and started debating with her. My eyes bounced back and forth between them as if I were watching my second sporting event of the week. And my presence was as irrelevant to them as it had been to the tiny football players on TV. The boy was extremely animated and matched the girls sequin for sequin. Eventually, I was folded into the conversation in the usual Lisboan fashion—with the conviction that the longer one speaks Portuguese, the more apt your foreign subject is to understand it. It's the Portuguese version of screaming English in order to better communicate. Everyone knows that works.

The three of them convened. They were an unusually good-looking bunch, even caked in makeup. I looked at the girls' heart-shaped faces and the boy's sloping nose. Each had a look of the purebred that many Americans find appealing, colony of mutts that we are. The boy flicked up his top hat as he leaned in to hear his female companions. I noticed the second girl was wearing two different types of shoes—a feather-covered high heel and a flat moccasin. I scanned up her legs, trying to compute how she was able to stand evenly.

I shook my head from face to face like a rotating fan. They were my sideshow freaks, and I was theirs. But they were growing frustrated with my lack of fluency. I wondered: did I speak English at the same speed they spoke Portuguese? It seemed unlikely. You know, I wanted to tell them, Portugal and Brazil may be the only hubs of your tongue in this world, but this is a language that's out there. I mean, it's around. The chances of there being more Portuguese to speak tomorrow are very good. No need to get it all out now.

"Wait, wait." I flipped my book open to the blank papers at the end. I sketched a quick map of the earth, using the kind of sloppy squiggling that makes Florida the size of Italy. In the circle I drew the picture I had in my head when I came here: that of a plane going from New York to Lisbon, leaving a dotted line in its wake. It looked smaller on the page than it had in my head.

"Naway Yorkah!" said the boy.

When they managed to ask me what I was doing there, I drew two equally sized figures: one a stick drawing of myself and the other a full glass of ink-colored wine. Pushing the book aside, I supplemented my sketch with the universal hand gesture for "sucking back the sauce." They looked concerned. The boy huddled his eyebrows together. I worried that he might cry real tears, ruining the perfectly rendered one already painted on his cheekbone. On him, I imposed a backstory of his entire clown family dying in a clown car pileup. He was then raised by some unfunny guardian who drank too much and beat him with the lion-taming crop and made him work the cotton-candy mills. Now even the faintest suggestion of substance abuse takes him back to his days spinning sugar, wishing his alkie clown overlord would choke on his foam nose.

"No, no." I drew three wineglasses in a row, circled them, and drew a hard line across the glasses.

"NOT AN AL-CO-HOL-IC," I enunciated, dragging the pen back and forth.

Relieved, they settled in. The girls rearranged the wire skeletons beneath their skirts. The boy brushed aside his jacket tails and relaxed. And we proceeded to play Pictionary at a third-grade level. When I ran out of margins, the second girl ran up to the bar and returned triumphantly with a fistful of fresh cocktail napkins. It's amazing what you can glean from people by doodling. Using stick figures to represent themselves, I learned that they were in fact in clown college. Not in addition to regular school but with the specific intent of becoming professional clowns. A topic they took very seriously.

In the most elaborate doodle of the night, they asked me to join them for their dress-rehearsal clown practice. It was just down the street. There would be comedy sketches. And fire swallowing. Or maybe blow jobs, the sign language for which is practically identical. There was also a party for one of their classmates, just back from the hospital after an unfortunate altercation between a tightrope and his groin.

"Never play leapfrog with a unicorn, huh?" I asked under my breath.

They ignored me and kept drawing, interrupting each other with gobs of Portuguese. By the time they finished, their doodle looked like an early sketch for *The Scream*. Overlaid with an early sketch for a three-ring orgy.

"Frankly, there's just not enough midget sodomy in this

picture," the first girl instructed the boy, "and ask yourself: is that really where cotton candy is meant to go?"

"It melts in more places than your mouth," said the boy, defending his contribution.

For all I knew they were just discussing the weather. They rotated the paper on the table without picking it up, their row of smiling faces like telephone wires.

Would I like to see a three a.m. performance of amateur Portuguese circus clowns? Oh, no, thank you. I declined for the same reason that I had run from the man in the alley. For the same reason I flew to Lisbon to watch hours of QVC porn. The freedom of being an adult, that condition which landed me here to begin with, came with a heavy price. I was beholden to no one. My family and friends back home had flight numbers and dates, sure, but I could be absolutely anywhere. Or, as my father used to put it, "dead in a ditch on the side of the road." As opposed to all the ditches built in the centers of roads. Point was: who were these clowns? If I went with them, I could wind up in a basement somewhere, unable to call for help in the proper language. Or, knowing Lisbon, the catacombs beneath the cellar beneath the basement.

However, with each glass of wine, our communication morphed from frustrating to liberating. The stick figures became increasingly elaborate, bordering on perverse. They went through puberty, developing scalloped breasts and generous crotchal endowments. It was enough to make you wish all human relations could be boiled down like this. We should all have to carry around paper-doll versions of ourselves, pointing to what hurts, pointing to what doesn't. It was like those ridiculous ABC *After School Specials* on AIDS and child abuse and class warfare, the ones that made *Degrassi High* look like quality programming.

"Show me, Suzy," said a permed and frost-tipped child psychologist. "Show me on the doll where the bad man touched you."

And Suzy would point. And the adult in the room would nod. And Suzy's hair would get tousled, because everything was going to be okay. She didn't have to be afraid anymore. How nice that must be, I always thought. Not the scarred-for-life or my-stepfather-is-up-for-parole part. But the part where you could momentarily explain all your vital information with the extension of an index finger. All you have to do is point, and with the speed of a near-death montage, every issue in your life is transferred to the closest listener. For a brief moment, the brain you've made such a mess of is someone else's problem. Here, you take this. I've been living with this model for thirty years, and I don't know what to do with it anymore.

"Okay," I said.

"Okay?" asked the girls in unison.

I pointed at the surrealist orgy sketch and made a walking gesture with my fingers. There's no such thing as a stockpile of missed opportunities. You just have to trust that the world knows what it's doing when it sends a bunch of circus freaks your way. Also, I had never seen cotton candy used like that before.

"Okay, I'll go with you."

They embraced one another and then me. We had time for one final round before clown practice, and I watched my first friend's eyes flicker beneath her beanie bangs. A wry smile came over her face. She grabbed my book and pinched the acknowledgments page, poised to tear it out.

"*Si?*" She looked at me.

"Go for it." I nodded.

She clutched the pen and scribbled, blocking the others with her elbow. When she was done, she revealed a doodle-confession regarding an affair with her teacher (a stick figure with a pipe in his mouth and extra-large clown shoes). The second girl muttered something to the effect of "No, *you* shut up." The first spoke in Portuguese but continued to draw at the same time, as if employing a type of sign language for my benefit. Closed Captioning for the American Tourist. She slung her arm around my shoulders, keeping me on her side as the bedlam unfolded. She felt possessive of me. I was her discovery, just as Lisbon was mine.

This, finally, was something I understood. People who have spent time in Lisbon talk about the city as if it's theirs. The city allows for this sense of possession in a way that more heavily trafficked places do not. If you are in Lisbon in December, it is very possible to walk past a store window, knowing that it will not host another reflection for whole hours. It is possible to look out onto the river and feel that you are the only one to look at it this way for centuries. And it is possible to be minding your own business and accidentally befriend a monolingual home-wrecking lady clown and her band of merry mimes.

The boy refused to believe her. He jumped up from the table while holding down his top hat to keep it from flying off from shock. To emphasize her point, the girl decided to take things to the next dimension. With her nails, she tore around the figure representing herself and the figure representing the teacher. She circled the crotches of each person, picked them up, and rubbed them together until the paper thinned to shreds. Then she put the shreds in her mouth and swallowed the whole affair with a big gulp of wine.

Lost in Space

Things were better during my genius years. I was eighteen months old when my mother found me in the living room with a pile of building blocks—counting and spelling as I stacked them. This wunderkind behavior continued, and as it is with oddities in children and the mothers who birthed them, mine called a medical professional. My mother spoke about my rate of development. She had recently read a drugstore novel about a super-genius test-tube baby who, moments out of the womb, had mastered blinking and staring at fixed objects. Granted, the baby went on to manipulate people with his mind, using his parents as puppets for world domination. But if drugstore-novel baby was any sort of barometer, I would be doing quadratic equations with my Cray-Pas by the end of the week. Tests were done. Psychologists were consulted. Special schools were researched. Should I be put in genius-kid school? Should I skip a grade? Two? Better wait a while and see if she "evens out," said the doctor. And he was right. While my parents doted on me, overzealously plying me with brain food and brainteaser games, a healthy case of the stupids kicked in, offsetting my block-building brilliance.

Blind to my sluggish development, my mother cried "genius" to anyone who would listen. All the while wiping away my doltish spittle while I swatted at her necklaces and played with my belly button.

By the time I was old enough to go to the bathroom on my own, I was just like every other kid. Maybe a little bright, but nothing to necessitate a lampshade. When it came to bedtime reading, I was less moon, more bowl full of mush. I also wet my bed, once mistook a wax candle for candy, and habitually banged my head so hard against the wall while I slept that my father installed padding. I was out of the woods.

Then one day, after years of mediocrity, all the kids in my grade were told we'd have to take a test on Iowa. I tried to piece together everything I knew about this subject, but I was eleven years old and my brain was like a slot machine: I put in "Iowa," pulled the lever, and it came up all corn. When at last the test landed on my desk, I found that "the Iowas" was the name of a basic skills test, the standard-ized kind administered to public-school kids. I assumed the test was concocted by someone in the Midwest for whom the question "If Suzy has twenty bales of hay and Jimmy borrows a bale per month until the frost, how many bales does Suzy have left?" was not hypothetical. I thought I did okay. In reality I bombed, landing in a breathtakingly low, of-the-masses percentile. The school called, expressing grave concern. Had all that unconscious head banging finally caught up with me? Should I be held back a grade? Two? In one section of the test, we had to look at a series of everyday objects, match them with their proper names, and fill in the bubbles on a Scantron sheet. I got nineteen out of thirty wrong.

"Sloane doesn't know what a spatula is," the school psychologist offered. The "Need I say more?" was silent.

"*Oh, please,*" said my mother. With the new cordless phone in one hand and my wrist in the other, she marched me to the kitchen, flung open a drawer, and held a rubber paddle in front of my face.

"This," she said, loudly enough for the school psychologist to hear, "is a spatula. Okay?"

"Okay." I nodded.

My mother went on to explain my brush with brilliance, my aptitude for genius, my general awesomeness, but the school was having none of it. They insisted I take an IQ test. The test was a combination of oral logic questions, written analogies, and pictures of deformed animals with missing hooves and otherworldly trees that failed to cast shadows. There would have to be something profoundly wrong with you to look at a one-legged donkey and see nothing amiss with that picture. But my cockiness took an instant beating with the math portion of the exam. Even the school psychologist was stunned, and she expressed her surprise by helping me cheat.

"How many people do you think there are in the world?" she read from a clipboard.

"A billion?" I bid on humanity.

"Oh, come *on*." She raised her thumb as if I was lowballing her.

Even with her help, I failed spectacularly. After getting gold stars on the first half of the test, I think she thought I was intentionally trying to throw the math section. For what purpose, I do not know. I was not raised in a movie where it's better to be a dumb jock than a bookish band geek. It was better to just be a super-hot band geek.

The psychologist informed my parents that she had rarely seen such a right-left brain discrepancy. At least not in kids who made it through the day without soiling themselves in public. And with that I was diagnosed with a severe temporal-spatial deficit, a learning disability that means I have zero spatial-relations skills. It was official: I was a genius trapped forever in an idiot's body. The reason I did so poorly on the Iowas was that the questions were multiple choice and presented vertically. Once I had decided on an answer (say, "spatula"), I had to remove my eyes from the paper and shade in the corresponding choice in a horizontal line of bubbles. This, much like reading a map, playing cards, or telling time on an analog clock, was an impossibility for me. The chances of my ever achieving a non-embarrassing level of mathematical functionality were about as good as the chances of Jimmy's returning those bales of hay.

My teachers were told to be sensitive about this, but my mother, armed with a biased skepticism and a master's in special education, started testing me at home. Just to be sure. She'd tell me to get something that was to the right or to the left of something else. She quickly discovered that I had already found ways of masking my panic—saying I was distracted while I was actually desperately trying to figure out the answer. I could feel her staring at the back of my head. I spent a lot of time like this, faking daydreams while counting or trying to guess which way is west if this way is north.

Another thing about having the village idiot camped out in half your brain is that the other half is forced into some resourceful public-relations work. At school, if someone asked me what time it was, the better-brain half would put its hand over the lesser half's mouth, and I'd say my watch was broken. Or I'd wear some numberless, handless, spinning-faced gadget on which no one with human eyes could tell time. The lies we construct to defend ourselves from humiliation are the strongest, refusing to be torn down. To this day, I've never met a clock that works properly. I think there's something faulty with the way they make the hands these days. Something in the screws, maybe. But who needs a watch when you have a cell phone? Problem solved.

By age twelve, I started wearing a bracelet on my left

wrist so I could look down and associate it with that direction. At the age of sixteen, I discovered it would take me twice as long as my peers to drive anywhere. No matter what part of town I happened to find myself in, I was swinging past my house between destinations to reorient myself. The good news was that my visual memory became stronger. I could tell you what you wore two weeks ago. I could memorize the internal organs of a fetal pig. I could sketch the contents of my locker in accurate detail—I just couldn't find it.

Flunking more of my classes than not, I was placed in an all-grade after-school program called The Learning Center. Which was purposefully veiled in a maze of confusion by the school's architects. "Center," I will say, was totally misleading. Perpetually late, I usually found that the only seats available were next to a mute paraplegic girl whose hair was done in bows, or the prematurely sexualized kid who told our teacher he'd like to "bone the fuck" out of her. Each week I sat next to the girl and read for an hour, handing her colored pencils and waiting for someone to ask me if I needed help with my homework. I declined. I didn't want to look stupid in front of the other kids.

Around this time, a couple of teachers broached the possibility of my taking my SATs orally. Throughout high school, they had slyly allowed me to circle my answers on the tests themselves, forgoing the Scantron sheet. Being a teenager is hard enough without having people look over at your exam paper to see an insane pattern of misplaced carbon dots in the margins. You know who else does that? Disaffected psychopaths in laced boots and trench coats.

But the SATs were bigger than high school. They plugged you into the rest of the nation. They ingrained a sense of patriotism that the chin-ups on the President's Physical Fitness Challenge had failed to do. In suburban New York, your life began in earnest once you took the SATs. They were the first determining factor for the next four years, a canary into the mines of your future. A dead canary, and you were looking at a nail-polish-merchandising degree from Pump My Stomach State. So, the nightmare of having to think out loud in the midst of all that pressure, to change your mind, to search someone else's face for signs of your rightness . . . It was too much. Instead, I sat with my mother in the same spot where she had once found me stacking blocks, and we devised a plan. I would write each answer on a Post-it note. Then I would unstick the note from the test, stick it to the answer sheet, and reread it while I made the correct mark. Not permitted to bring outside materials into the exam room, I padded my bra with Post-it notes. The proctors were accustomed to no end of odd teenage behavior. They said nothing when I periodically scratched my strangely square breasts.

This worked well enough to get me into college. But it couldn't work every day. I was living in the movie *Labyrinth*, but without the evil-puppet factor. I have never outgrown that feeling of constant disorientation. Rather, the feeling has followed me around like a homing device.

I finally came to terms with this when I was returning home from college the Thanksgiving of my freshman year. My father and I stopped off at a sprawling Connecticut market with curving aisles and outdoor spaces and multiple entrances. We split up. When I had collected the items on my half of the list, I tried to find him. For fifteen minutes, I circled back through the crowds and around shortcuts that landed me in places I had just left. I was at a loss. Should I ask someone to lead me to the manager's office, where I could call my father over the PA system? I once heard that you can find your way out of any maze by keeping your hand on the left side of the wall. Great, but which side was left? Damn you, David Bowie. Maybe I could live here, mopping and stocking my way to room and board. Eventually I gave up beneath a sign for *Festive Pumpkins!*, thinking it was best to stay put until my father found me.

It was the indignity of it all that bothered me. Consequence-wise, the experience of getting lost is not the end of the world. Unless you do it imprudently, veering toward poorly lit parking garages and uncovered manholes, nothing terrible beyond tardiness is going to happen to you. But that's the thing. A learning disability doesn't exactly qualify as an emergency. It's a subtle problem for everyone except the person who has it. Standing in the middle of the aisle with the shoppers buzzing around me, I told myself

I would trade breaking a bone just once rather than continue with a lifetime of this crap. Because at least with a broken bone you get a cast or a sling. People see your problem coming. But how do you explain an eighteen-year-old trapped and teary-eyed in front of a pile of seasonal gourds? Where is her excuse?

It would get a little better as I became an adult. I learned my right from my left and my up from my down. Unfortunately, that school psychologist, in defiance of the grand tradition of incompetent childhood professionals, turned out to be correct about my functionality cap. Even now, I do all public counting with one fist under the table, preferably in a jacket pocket. If there is no pocket to be had, I twitch my knuckles instead of fully extending my fingers. It's less obvious that way. And I still can't tell time on an analog clock. Or, rather, I can, but it takes me ten minutes, a lapse that defeats the purpose of the exercise. This remains unbelievable to most people, as demonstrated by the well-meaning but misguided response, "I'll teach you right now!" *Oh, no, really, I . . . Okay, let's get this over with.* I try to avoid the kitchens in other people's apartments, as this is where most analog wall clocks live, and apparently there are few activities so fun as herding a cocktail party full of people into one room to watch a grown woman try to tell time. Of course, age grants you a whole new set of loopholes. *You mean that wall clock there? Sorry, I can't read shit without my glasses.*

My terrible sense of direction also remains. To live in

New York City is to never be able to meet someone on the northeast corner. It is to never, ever make a smooth entrance, always getting caught looking lost on the street. The only subway I can exit and begin striding forth with confidence is the one by my home, as there is a gigantic park on the right-hand side. And I know I don't live in the trees with the pigeons and the butterflies. Otherwise, I always go the wrong direction. The trains were slow, I complain, when in actuality the trains were fine and I went the wrong way down Broadway. Again. I dated someone who lived near the Seventh Avenue stop in Brooklyn, and an odd phenomenon occurred every time I'd visit. When I left his apartment, I'd go into the subway through the same entrance. The next time I arrived, I'd find the entrance, go up the familiar staircase, and it spat me out across the street from where I needed to be. I have no idea why. *We're all mad here, says the Cheshire Cat. I'm mad. You're mad. . . .*

It's not a disability, it's life. We are complicated creatures with larger matters on our plates than tip calculation. I grew up watching TV with my mother while she diagnosed the characters as having hyperactivity or attention-deficit disorder. I rolled my eyes and wondered why there weren't any stupid kids anymore. Why did there have to be something to explain everyone? Were the cave people on Ritalin? I didn't think so.

But waiting for my father to find me in the supermarket that day, I started calculating how many times I had embarrassed myself, how many perfectly functional watch faces I had defamed. Whatever natural inability I had to orient myself I had doused with a self-made need to cover it up. People get lost and invert numbers. They make plans for Tuesday the sixteenth when the sixteenth is a Wednesday. Most people would claim they are "terrible with" something. Names, dates, faces. Even make-believe characters on TV had these problems. But did they feel the need to lie about them afterward?

WHEN I CONFESSED MY SAT METHODS TO A FRIEND, she said she knew someone who had facial blindness, a kind of recognition agnosia that makes it impossible for her to recall faces of casual acquaintances and old friends. To compensate, she goes through life taking photographs and being dangerously friendly to strangers on the street. *How cool,* I thought. If anything, this is a convenient way to snub people. I also found this woman's existence oddly reassuring. I wondered how many of us there were out there with severe disabilities walking among us, like anti–X-Men with disadvantageous powers.

Recently, my sister had a barbecue, and the best means of getting to her house is to take the bus. I took the opportunity to leave the country for the weekend instead.

"We were making fun of you," my mother recounted.

"I thought, *She's going to Canada because she doesn't want to take the bus.*"

"No one would go to Canada over that, Mom. It's a ladies' weekend in Montreal."

"You can't fool me," she said. "I know how much you hate the bus."

"Mother, I feel as strongly about the bus as I do about the Canadians."

"No," she reveled in her rightness, "I think you'd rather sit on a Canadian than on a bus."

"Well, sure," I gave in. "That's probably true."

Fine, I thought. *Let them think I'm a snob. Let them think I'm lazy. See if I care.* It's better than the fear of falling down the rabbit hole and realizing the smiling cat has a better sense of direction than you do, and then running into the white rabbit only to realize that *he* has facial agnosia and doesn't recognize you, and it's not as if you can read his pocket watch, anyway.

Then my mother, forever the parent of a genius toddler, laughed and said, "But I know you, and I thought, She won't get on a bus because it'll take her too long to translate the schedule. And then she won't know which direction to go when she gets off. And then I thought, I wish I could tell her that it's no problem—I'll just stand at the corner, and when she walks down the stairs I'll be there to meet her."

Take a Stab at It

A week before college graduation, I made plans to live in New York with my friend Mac. Mac's parents were intent on buying him an apartment. The idea was for them to pay the mortgage and for me to pay the monthly maintenance. On average, we were talking about a good four hundred dollars less than renting from scratch. Though not the real estate equivalent of winning the lottery, it was certainly the equivalent of finding a bunch of money on the street and keeping it. Over the next few months, most of the New York–bound members of our graduating class had also paired off—or, in some cases, quadrupled off—erecting fake walls out of bookshelves and pounding the underdeveloped fishy quadrants of Red Hook, tearing phone numbers off the paper fringe on lampposts. They divided spaces that were never meant to be divided. It was like splitting a wasabi pea in half with your thumb. Doors opened into bed corners more often than not. Watching TV was a bet with gravity, as sets hung from the ceiling for want of shelf space. Flat screens existed, but they were prohibitively expensive for the people who needed them most, people who needed their heads uninjured and their hallways unblocked. All immediate hints of purpose went out of the rooms themselves. Showers in kitchens, toilets in living rooms, sinks in bedrooms. It was as if Picasso were born a slumlord instead of a painter. Nothing was where you thought it would be, which would be eccentric in a mansion but was disarming in an apartment. Once, at a party, I opened a door expecting to find a toilet but found a stove instead. Just a closet with a stove in it. And a bare bulb hanging, as if to say, "Here is where we roast the children."

Meanwhile, Mac and I were taking tours of rooms that made sense, in apartments with full-on hallways. I took the train in from Westchester, dreaming of where I'd meet Mac and his parents next. Home was just around the corner. I had set sail on a little ship called *Sponsorship*, part of the Fleet of Parental Enablement. The horizon of happiness was as clear and measured a line as the walls that met the floors without wobbling. Mac and I could even pick the neighborhood, a fantasy I indulged by going on real estate websites and hovering my giant arrow over the lower portions of Manhattan. I amused myself with the concept that there would be a "minimum" a tenant could pay. I liked to imagine myself as one half of a couple, both of us in panther-skin shoes, storming out of a converted candy warehouse upon discovering that it was too cheap. It was all very *Brewster's Millions.*

And, oh, the apartments I saw! The appliances gleamed in defiance of our slovenly and disaffected youth. Faucets arced up from the backs of sinks, stopping in midair to fan out wide. They seemed more comfortable in the world than I did. I understood I was about a decade too early to live a life in which I casually washed my hands in freestanding square sinks. There were living rooms with dark wooden floors and vaulted bedrooms with skylights. A few of the apartments were duplexes with winding staircases that led us to roof decks, where upon arrival our broker would apologize for an archway covered in roses.

"We can get rid of this." She'd gesture at the problem without deigning to look at it. "You are a person of importance, and if you want us to behead flowers for you, we'll gladly do it."

I knew I could be a healthy, successful, content person in these apartments. And Mac knew it, too. I could see it in his face. We would be generous with our friends—come, use our rooftop sauna! Come, pull up a stool to the kitchen island and drink our small-batched liquor! Spend the night in a room with a door! But when they left, we would have the secret to life: all the perks of comfortable adulthood and all the joie de vivre of people who eschewed landlines and partook of Scorpion Bowls. Like polar bears in the Arctic, our friends were content to float on blocks of ice no bigger than their butts. But Mac and I were destined for something greater. A refrigerator taller than our hips, for instance. As we toured apartment after apartment together, me happily playing the role of stray animal, all I thought about was that my bedroom would have a knob that was housed in a door that was housed in a wall that was housed in a building that probably wouldn't fall down. What else could I need?

There were, as there almost always are, signs this was never going to work. As it was with the leaking Red Hook ceilings I had narrowly avoided sleeping under, the cracks were beginning to show. I was dealing with normal people. In situations like this, it's best to deal with the obscenely rich or the obscenely stupid. Preferably both. But Mac's was a more-than-nice family of more-than-moderate intelligence. They rationalized an additional mortgage as an investment. At heart, they were not a buy-my-grown-child-an-apartment kind of people. Though . . . at one point they did express concern that their freshly minted adult would be sleeping on a futon. They went on and on about the ramifications of this, both physical and psychological. Apparently, footing the entire bill for his housing glided down a separate stream of consciousness, a ship with no raised flags. But a futon? How juvenile.

The problem began with the fuzzy moral area of contributing to someone else's mortgage, knowing your short-term funds were being poured into their long-term venture. With

each apartment we viewed, my contribution incremen-
tally increased. For a while this was an easily overlooked
dilemma. I was still paying less than I would have on my
own, and I was not particularly concerned with their financial compartmentalization. I had no concept of how long it
took to actually purchase and move into a home (months)
vs. how long it took to rent one (seconds, depending on
how fast you could sign your name and throw an elbow at
the prospective tenant coming up the stairwell behind you).
Before the economy imploded, renting in Manhattan was a
boxing match between how you were raised and how much
money you had from week to week. You would pay and do
just about anything for a livable space. A room of one's
own was probably not in the cards, but a bamboo folding
screen might be nice. As you flipped through the backs of
local magazines en route to the crossword, you'd find yourself hovering for a moment over the escort agency ads and
thinking, *How bad would that really be?* And with thoughts
like these in the mix, the lesser moral infractions seemed less
infractiony. In this corner, measuring all the life you've led
by all the life you have yet to lead, weighing the sum total of
your sense of right and wrong, is your Morality. And in that
corner, containing a twenty-dollar bill and a half-stamped
coffee card, is . . . And we're done.

Plus, Mac was my friend. Friendship is a Spackle in itself.
You'll forgive your friends a lot, and if you're a woman,
you'll forgive your straight male friends even more. They

represent the possibility of mutual toleration between the sexes, a keyhole into the mind of the Other, and the promise of one day meeting someone just like them except that you want to sleep with them.

The situation became palpably tense as Mac's parents began to feel a sense of unfairness that I would be paying so little each month, even with the steady increases in my contribution. It was not a buyer's market. Mortgages would have to be recalculated. Bathrooms would have to be retiled. Places were too small or too dark or too far away from the subway—a henna tattoo of a problem for a renter but a more enduring concern for a buyer. As their comfort faltered, unsubtle suggestions that I contribute more were floated my way.

"They think you should pay more," said Mac.

"How much more is more?"

We had long since blown past the monthly maintenance mark. We had doubled it. And yet, miraculously, the dimensions of my closet remained the same. I was a second-class citizen paying first-class prices. One evening, after his parents had gone back to their world of doormen and digital cable, I offered to buy Mac a slice of pizza. I put down our tiny cups of water and reached for my wallet. The only cash I had on me was a one-dollar bill.

"Don't worry about it," Mac said. "You'll get me next time."

But I *was* worried about it. Disproportionately so. He

wasn't the one with the frowning face of George Washington folded into the fetal position in his back pocket. If I felt this indebted over pizza, how was I going to cope with floor-to-ceiling French doors? I could feel the resentment bubble. Not like a cheese bubble, which is very noticeable, but like a little pocket of raw guilt heating into something altogether different, something that muttered, *You're not even paying rent, asshole, your parents are.*

I had to get out. I cited my own impatience with suburbia and my call time at my first job, which remained stubbornly at eight-thirty a.m. ten months into it. I couldn't keep waking up before sunrise to get to the train station, deactivating the alarm in my parents' house like I was in high school. It wasn't him, he had to understand, it was me. Maybe we could, you know, try to see other roommates. Fortunately, Mac accepted this. But it was too late. I had watched all my other viable roommate options, those vetted by the four-year background check called "college," chip off the real estate glacier. I was stranded. So I turned to that mecca of desperation, the Internet. But instead of tormenting myself with panoramic videos of views I'd never witness from balconies I'd never stand on, I went on Craigslist and found Nell.

Nell was a closet anorexic and a casual kleptomaniac. Neither affliction you'd think would be a problem when considered carefully. For starters, I'd never have to worry about her eating my food. Indeed, on more than one occasion

I'd be brushing my teeth and she'd appear in the bathroom door with two versions of the same product in each hand.

"See, my peanut butter has more carbs"—she'd raise one container like a barbell, her parenthesis of an arm muscle straining from the process—"but your peanut butter has more saturated fat."

Our refrigerator was becoming a condiment ark. We had two of just about everything. It was like we were kosher but instead of doing it out of piety, we were doing it out of hostility. I would turn to face her in slow motion, still brushing. And she'd wait for my reaction. Wait, brush, wait, brush. Until I'd spit and say something through the toothpaste foam like "That's a solid point you make" or "Yeah, I'm thinking about switching."

What can I say? Anorexics are very neat, and they pay their bills on time.

The kleptomania had also not been cause for concern. At least not at first.

A. None of my clothes would fit her without the aid of belts or a staple gun.

B. Her thievery was so open, I never had that panicky feeling that I'd left a sweater in the bar or lost it to the dry cleaner. A quick peek in her room would reveal the item, cuffs rolled up, laid tidily on her bed.

But what I hadn't taken into account were accessories. Nary a woman has bloated earlobes. Handbags, in particular, are one-size-fits-all.

The result was a lot of conversations that went like this:

"Nell, is that my necklace?"

"Yes," she'd say, touching her neck to confirm the fact.

"Where did you find it?"

"In your jewelry box."

It seemed ironic that someone who adamantly eschewed all street foods could possess such sticky fingers. If I bought clothing, I'd sneak the bags into the apartment. If I left for the weekend, I'd drop off my laundry at the laundromat beforehand to get my stuff off the premises. When Nell took a shine to my loofah, I started using a plastic shower caddy, which I made a big show of escorting from my bedroom to the bathroom each morning. Instead of growing into my first year of adulthood, I was reverting back to freshman year of college. It was a futon mentality.

Thus commenced a passive-aggressive note-leaving campaign in which I found myself doling out unwelcome life advice like the old man in the Werther's Original commercials. *Timmy, sometimes, when people own things, they like to keep track of them. And sharing is different from stealing, even if, as you say, I wasn't here to ask. . . . We're not possession-renouncing monks, Timmy, much as we'd like to be.*

Alas, the notes fell on deaf ears. Deaf ears with my earrings sticking through them. I found myself storing my grandmother's pendants in half-empty jars of fatty peanut butter.

Then came my big break. Nell packed up her Purell and

her Luna bars and left for a monthlong trip to Nepal to find herself spiritually. I felt as if I'd won an all-expenses-paid, all-nude-all-the-time vacation in my own home. Or at least the right to leave my headphones on the coffee table, safe in the knowledge they'd be there when I returned. Every roommate feels a sense of unexpected calm when they are given a reprieve from the mate and left with the room. It's not that you do anything more scandalous than walking around in ridiculous outfits, leaving cereal bowls in the sink, and smoking something low-grade out the window, but the air is filled with the idea that you *could* stay up all night blaring Hall & Oates, that you *could* sacrifice a live pigeon in the bathtub, that you *could* have a crazy scarf orgy in which you invite a bunch of people over and each person takes a scarf from your roommate's closet and has sex wearing their scarf of choice.

As the days rolled on, I grew accustomed to thinking of myself as someone with a guest room. I never entered the room—save for an initial ransacking sweep of my own possessions—but I liked to think of it like an annex. I decided her bedroom was like one of those preserved boudoirs you see on tours of Hyde Park or Versailles fitted with Plexiglas dead ends that will allow you in only so far, spaces you can walk into but not walk into.

One night, after too much eating-of-the-cereal and smoking-of-the-things-out-the-window, I tore up a card-board box and taped two panels to the inside of her door frame, with a third panel at the end. Then I took a long red ribbon and hung it limply with thumbtacks. I had just opened my laptop to create an ersatz historical plaque when my phone began to vibrate. I could hear it rumble beneath the surface of clothing and magazine sediment that had built up in the past week. I picked up on the swan-song ring. It was Mac. Mac, with whom I hadn't spoken since the Great Apartment Debacle of Four Months Ago. Mac, who caught me at the right moment. It is impossible to be angry and write fake museum-exhibit copy at the same time.

In the end, Mac's parents had purchased him a spacious alcove studio in Gramercy Park. Free of the uncomfortable albatross that was my presence, their generosity flourished. They agreed to pay both his rent and monthly maintenance in full. Which was really their rent in full, since their names were on the mortgage. Mac was bashful when I pressed for this information, which I already had. It had come to me through mutual friends. Friends who were, at this very moment, sharing greasy take-out food beneath duct-taped TV sets and laughing at each other's jokes. What Mac did tell me was how guilty he felt about what had happened between us, and that he, too, had been robbed of those innuendo-free nights of roommate bonding. He had been given a great gift, but with great gifts come very judgmental doormen.

Then he told me about an artist's loft he knew of. I protested, citing false loyalty to Nell. She would be unreachable for another two weeks. I couldn't have her come back to an apartment with my furniture cleared out and my closets empty. For Christ's sake, what would she wear? Of course, the real source of my hesitation was the phrase "artist's loft," which I took as a euphemism for "bad art" and "no heat." I knew even fewer successful artists than I did writers and musicians. I imagined a great deal of splatter paint and acrylic. Obscure animal hair. Maybe a couple of chairs that I would be scolded for defining as such. I also had questions about the legitimacy of the word "loft," which gets tossed around so easily when preceded by "artist's." Not all shabby is chic, just like not every porn actor is a star.

"But it's twenty-five hundred square feet," Mac said, a fact that in Manhattan inspires all acts short of murder. Even then, people have killed for less. Like fifteen-hundred-square-foot apartments. At twenty-five hundred square feet, I could do triple salchows. I could set up a full-sized tennis court and still have room for my bed behind the baseline. I would barely even have to *see* my roommate. We could be like an estranged couple who live under the same roof for the sake of appearances but confine themselves to their respective wings.

I looked around at my home. Modestly blueprinted, it was more like the set of a play than a place where humans actually lived. All four doors (front, bathroom, and two bedroom) opened onto the living room. The living room bled into the kitchen, separated only by a sheet of fake floor tile when you crossed over. Our one window faced a view-obscuring metal pole. I settled my gaze on my bedroom door. I remembered the time I found one of my Werther's Original notes retaped to the middle of the door. Nell had shoe-napped a pair of three-inch heels, leaving me to play Melanie Griffith in *Working Girl* for the day, my hosiery-encased feet slipping out of my Converses. Meanwhile, in an organic juice bar somewhere across town, my roommate was traipsing around in brand-new cow skin. That called for a note. When I returned home, I found Nell looking straight ahead at the TV and watching a show called *Movie and a Makeover*. She ate baked potato chips slowly and methodically, like a drugged-out woodchuck. The program did an impressive job of tying together *Sleepless in Seattle* with home spa recommendations. I tugged the paper down and approached Nell.

"But this doesn't apply to me," I offered.

"Well"—she perked up, snide and prepared—"you want everything back that's yours. The note is yours."

Mac was waiting for an answer. I put the pot in a drawer and the cereal bowl in the sink. I ripped down the ribbon, the thumbtacks rolling to some secret place between the floor-boards where one of them would retaliate by stabbing me in the toe two days later. On my laptop, I closed out of my museum copy without saving it, double-clicked on Netscape, and waited for my e-mail to open.

"Okay," I told him. "Send me the goods."

FOR A YOUNG RENTER, IT'S FAIRLY COMMON TO receive e-mails calling for roommates and sublets for unreasonably brief periods of time. *Fully furnished bedroom available in three-person apartment for January* and *February! Wait—and* February? Pinch me.

Unless you are a Japanese businessman, why anyone would desire an apartment furnished with someone else's crap escapes me. I don't know any Japanese businessmen. Nor, to my knowledge, do I know anyone who knows any Japanese businessmen. To whom are these e-mails directed? I don't feel entirely comfortable using someone else's Brita filter; forget sleeping on their mattress. There's also the odd specificity of these e-mails. The more detailed they are, the more they make me uncomfortable. It's the strange marriage of the personal and the practical. In New York, you can be reasonably good friends with someone for years and never see the inside of their apartment. It takes a year to narrow down their neighborhood.

You live in the West Village, right?

East.

Are you sure you don't live in Brooklyn? I find that hard to believe.

Believe it.

Well, Jane here lives in a studio in Hell's Kitchen.

No, I don't.

You don't?

I live in a two-bedroom with my boyfriend in Inwood.

Shut up. You're dating someone?

So, to be suddenly thrust into the space where casual acquaintances slap their alarm clocks each morning is to be given more information than your relationship requires. Yesterday you knew what department they worked in and whether they smoked cigarettes. Today you know where they get their coffee and prescription drugs, and that if you don't jiggle their toilet handle, the toilet will run all day. These descriptions are like an advertisement for the person as much as for the apartment. Their long-term costs, their dimensions, their quirks, their capacity to receive sunlight. Therefore, mystery is not the name of the game when sending out an apartment listing. Charm them with your cool-but-not-overtly-cloying language; let them know this is a safe place, a cool place; head all questions off at the pass. This listing was the opposite of that.

I double-clicked on the bold **"FW: INSANELY huge, available immediately/slightly flexible."** I marveled at my lax spam filter. The e-mail read as follows:

Roommate needed for artist's share

295 Bowery

washer/dryer

2,500 sq. ft.
$800 a month
Call. DO NOT BUZZ.

The whole thing was suspect. Not only did the e-mail lack details, but it was yelling at me. And eight hundred dollars a month? Eight hundred dollars a month was so amazingly gift-from-the-gods cheap that it aroused suspicion. I couldn't imagine what was wrong with this place, but it had to be something. Maybe there was no retaining wall. Maybe there were no walls, period. Just a converted pigeon coop and an intricate series of shower curtains. Perhaps if you buzzed, it disturbed the colonies of rats living under the floorboards? Meanwhile, I longed for the days when "artist's" was accompanied by "loft." A "loft" left you in peace; a "share" dead-fished you into a group hug. Would I have to participate in the artiness? I didn't feel a strong desire to paint canvases with beetle dung and fashion toothbrushes using human hair.

What hooked me in the end was the presence of a washer and dryer. People may not murder for twenty-five hundred square feet in Manhattan, but they'll maim for a washer and dryer. I typed the address into Google. I don't know what I was looking for. I didn't recall Mac implying anything special about the apartment beyond its dimensions. Perhaps I just wanted some insight into my potential neighbors. Maybe a résumé of some earnest MFA candidate or a male model's plea for the return of lost head shots. I didn't expect much. And certainly not the five hundred hits that came back to me. This was 2002. Five hundred hits was a lot in 2002. That would be like twenty thousand hits in today's Web currency.

But almost none of the hits concerned the building's current residents. I was scrolling through a virtual graveyard of newspaper archives and real estate websites, each link a headstone from the past. In the early twentieth century, 295 Bowery was a brothel. And not just any IHOP-style whorehouse. It was the site of the worst, and by default the most famous, brothel in the history of New York City: McGurk's Suicide Hall. A macabre tourist attraction a century ago, in one year no less than six prostitutes killed themselves because the conditions were so poor. Apparently the bartenders were on suicide watch, told to keep an eye out for nipple-exposed women standing in close proximity to pocket daggers, bottles of ether, open windows, that sort of thing. This must have been a conflicting assignment. It was in the best interest of the business's reputation for a percentage of these women to continue killing themselves.

I, however, experienced no such conflict of conscience. I would be sleeping with the ghosts of dead sluts! How could I resist? Here, finally, was my converted candy warehouse. Except that instead of an "a" in the warehouse there was a "ho." Several, actually.

I called immediately, eager for my first whore haunting. Presumably these were the vengeful brand of specter, the kind that refuses to move on. But I figured they'd be kind to me just for believing in them. And believe in them I did. I have seen too many movies about the paranormal. Too much bad dialogue has been exchanged; too much over-wrought acknowledgment of the ridiculous has been imbed-ded in phrases like "Oh my God, you guys! Did you hear that?" and "But Grandma's been *dead* for twenty years!" In the movies I'm thinking of, if the viewer's disbelief isn't sus-pended by act three, the director will forcefully bungee it off a bridge. There have been too many well-rendered special effects, too many starlets with flashlights under their faces muttering the mantra "I don't believe in ghosts," only to be told that their beliefs, like their thighs and knowledge of global politics, are nothing. Because the ghosts believe in them.

According to my Internet research, the apartment was one of only a handful of units. Two were occupied by a feminist activist known for her work, ironically, about sex and prostitution. The one I'd be visiting was under the ownership of a Canadian artist who, for reasons unknown, sublet the space for far less than it was worth. Occasionally, it seemed someone would get married or go back to grad school and then the apartment would be unhooked like a rare fish, released back into the Craigslist stream of other-wise untenable listings. A golden ticket with gills.

For these reasons, I began to think the apartment was calling to me. Even at the time, I knew that this sort of backstory was providing me with a false sense of destiny. Lots of people live in apartments with history in the floorboards. Usually it's obscure history having to do with famous people. Marilyn Monroe ate a hamburger in your lobby. Edgar Allan Poe once bought a pot of ink in your basement. But McGurk's Suicide Hall was the reverse—it was the anonymity, the relative uncommemoration of these women, that I found irresistible. No one knew their names, but everyone knew their profession. I also thought of what I'd be leaving. For all their paid promiscuity and suicidal tendencies, at least the ghosts of McGurk's disappeared the old-fashioned way. Whereas my current roommate was doing it by shedding body mass. The former seemed less gruesome somehow.

MY NEW ROOMMATE WAS A TALL KOREAN HIPSTER who answered the door in a man's flannel shirt. She had misjudged the button-to-hole alignment, leaving one swath of cloth farther below her belt than the other. But she couldn't be bothered to start over. She wore black jeans and no shoes. It was as if she knew the beer-bottle shards and cigarette butts and centuries of grime would bow in deference to the filth of her feet. And filthy they were, striking some shade between the matted nest of her hair and the oxidized toe ring that clung unhappily to her pinkie toe.

When she seemed surprised to see me, I knew instantly not to take it personally.

"Hey, I'm Sang," she said, looking into some middle distance between my face and hers. I wiped my nose. She cocked her head at me, and I cocked my head in the same direction.

"I'm Sloane. Mac's friend."

"Yeah. Come up," she added, as if I were the one holding us back.

As I followed her up the stairs, I thought of how strange it is to follow anyone up the stairs. Your face is so close to their butt. It's one of the unsung pleasures of riding in cabs—I have seen very little cabbie ass in my life. Whereas my fellow subway riders' cheeks are thrust, shifting back and forth, in front of me every day, countless as stars. Sang's ass was not so much an ass but a continuation of leg and bone, covered by pockets because society demanded it be covered by pockets. They came with the jeans. But much like the rest of Sang, her ass seemed inconvenienced to exist at all. I wondered about the build of the women who first ascended this staircase. People from one hundred years ago looked different. Rounder and smaller at the same time. More forehead, less chin. I am often curious about the texture of their hair. This is why period films are so unconvincing. Because actresses use conditioner and have been plucking their eyebrows for years, and you can't hire the dead.

A few beat-up sepia photos of the women from the last century hung, warped, in cracked frames drilled into the brick. They wore boots and feathers and stared with purpose into a bulky wooden box to have their portrait taken. I imagined them lifting their skirts as they marched up these same steps, a red-faced drunk in my position—bob, shift, bob, shift, mustache, mustache, bowler hat. Of course, the kind of women walking up these steps would not likely be wearing skirts long enough to lift.

"So, how long have you lived here?" I said to the ass.

"Don't know," the ass threw its voice. "A while now, I guess."

I wondered what it must be like for the lucky gent who dated Sang. It's never good to fall in love with someone whom you'd have to stab in the eyeballs to elicit a response. Sang pushed the metal door with a callused heel, and it swung inward with surprising ease.

There are fulcrum moments in life when you can feel your world pivot in a new direction. Everything that mattered doesn't. There is no adjustment period between the old and the new. Slice open the plastic bag and pour the goldfish straight into the bowl. Here is how your life will go from now on. My moment came while looking at the dining room table in Sang's loft. I would make as many toothbrushes out of hair as the situation required if I could do it at that dining room table.

Crafted in the "picnic" school of tables, complete with benches, it had been rescued from a flea market in Norway, painted white, and then intentionally stripped so that swirling knots of wood overpowered the paint. It was oversized and smooth. Above it hung a chandelier with every other bulb covered by a plastic doll's head. Brunettes and blondes and a redhead glowed from their eye sockets. There's no way to convince someone that a doll-head chandelier is tasteful. But this one was. As I strolled around the place, I kept alert for signs of crafts or splatter paint or batiking of any kind. But all I found were beautiful touches that put the creative solutions necessitated by my small space to shame. Like the refrigerator sunk into the wall and then painted to match the wallpaper. Or the slab of jagged marble on the back of the toilet to replace the porcelain cover. It was a beautifully disheveled mess. A warmer, more cared-for version of Andy Warhol's Factory. There was even a potted tree of some kind, and it was more or less alive. This, despite Sang's repeated attempts to kill it.

"I never water that thing," said Sang, "but it just keeps on living."

We sat on one of the artfully mismatched sofas surrounding a freestanding fireplace. I sank into the cushion until it touched the floor.

"Also, there's no air-conditioning," she said, looking down with superhuman vision to remove one of her hairs from her black jeans. "I mean, obviously. It's a loft."

Did I look like the kind of girl who was going to storm in, demanding Freon? I was; I just didn't want to look like it.

"Oh, that's okay," I said, picturing my practically medieval collection of hair-torturing devices. On hot days, I had been known to stick my freshly burned scalp in the freezer. I was willing to eschew it all if I lived here. I would be the kind of girl who doesn't blow-dry her hair, who has transcended the brush.

"And," she continued, "there's no hot water. There is, but it's two seconds and then it turns freezing cold."

"Good!" I clapped my hands. "Must offset the humidity!"

She could have told me that the mattresses were full of bedbugs and I was going to have to sleep on plastic sheets, and I would have clapped like a trained seal.

We sat in silence. I listened to the traffic on Houston, trying to determine if it would be worse or better at night as I fell asleep in my envy-inducing bedroom.

"How is it that this place is available?"

Sang explained her situation—a bad boyfriend whom she had kicked out. She described him as "one of those non-talkative types."

"Some people are just so blasé about everything." Sang sighed.

I said that yes, I had heard of such a person.

Then I explained my situation—a bad roommate I described as one of those "non-eating types." When I men-

tioned the casual kleptomania, Sang perked up for the first
time. Stealing was something to which she could relate. You
could really picture her hanging out with open thieves, tir-
ing of people she called "friends" stealing her credit cards
and photocopying her passport. Not cool, guys. Not cool.
So I delved further, but too deep too fast, uttering more syl-
lables through normal conversation than Sang had released
in the past week. The more I detailed Nell's crimes, the more
Sang distanced herself from me.

"So, she wears your stuff without asking? Oh. I guess
that can be annoying. I grew up with sisters, so—"

"So did I!" I attempted to sit up straight, but the couch
pulled me back. "But this girl isn't my sister."

I did a quick mental montage of every time I had
attempted to borrow an article of clothing from my sister in
high school. Not one image featured her giving it to me of
her own volition. Indeed, several featured locked drawers
and slammed doors and, in one instance, a thrown Walk-
man. I stole from her as a matter of habit. But Sang didn't
need to know this.

What she needed to know was that the first time I laid eyes
on Nell was in a broker's office. We were then chaperoned
by a landlord showing us an apartment. Nell kept removing
nuts from a plastic bag in her pocket and seemed concerned
with installing motion sensors in the grateless windows, but
I didn't mind because I thought, *Well, it's good to snack, and*

I don't know why I don't carry around nuts more often. And New York is a dangerous place. Why should homeowners have a monopoly on protecting their bodies and their valuables with silent alarms? Desperation is a funny thing, I explained to Sang, who seemed never to have experienced the sensation. Rarely does it announce itself. It is instead the silent killer of expectations until you don't think of yourself as desperate. You think of yourself as a reasonable person who compromises because that's what living with a room-mate is about, compromise. . . .

I was losing her. She was lost in thought, looking me up and down. I strummed my knees to fill the silence.

"I like your picnic table." I pointed.

"It's not mine." She looked with me.

"That's cool." I nodded.

When Sang escorted me to the door, I wasn't sure how to say good-bye. A hug, a handshake, and direct eye contact were equally out of the question. This woman made me feel naked. Luckily, I had clothes on, so I opted to jam my fingers into my pockets and sway. On the street, cars honked in frustration, trying to get to the FDR. Sang leaned against the thick door frame.

"It's quiet at night," she said.

"Even with the ghosts?"

"What ghosts?"

"I read somewhere that this place used to be an old

brothel. Apparently, a bunch of prostitutes threw themselves out the window."

"My God." Sang covered her mouth. "That's horrible!"

"It's sad."

"No." She wrapped the bones of her hand around my arm. "That's so horrific."

"Well"—I didn't know how to handle this level of alertness—"it's certainly *whore*-ific, I'll give you that."

Sang was not amused. Figures. The one time I'm cavalier about a subject and I'm underreacting. Certainly throwing oneself out the window is objectively worse than borrowing a bra without asking. But most people tended to have Sang's reaction to Nell's tendencies.

"Haven't you ever noticed the pictures in the stairwell?" I asked Sang.

I knew making her feel foolish was probably not the key to her steely heart, but how could she not know? I didn't expect her to turn into an Asian Scooby-Doo, but surely there was a baseline level of curiosity all humans shared. Food, shelter, clothing, creepy old shit. New Yorkers in particular are masochists when it comes to obtaining housing information that will only piss them off. We are gluttons for discovering that our twenty-unit apartment building used to be a single-family home. And not even a nice one at that.

"Huh," she mused. "I thought they were from a thrift shop or something."

———

I RETURNED TO MY APARTMENT AND LOOKED AT MY bedroom, which felt smaller than ever. Every inch was planned and decorated because I had no choice. I looked in Nell's bedroom. Everything was so neat and perfectly matched. I felt myself falling somewhere between Nell and Sang. I could sense them both categorizing me as the other when they looked at me, a feeling that made me wish I could put them in the same room together and say, "You think *I'm* bad? Look at *this*!"

Mentally, I was already packing, deciding what I'd bequeath to Nell when she returned from Nepal and what I'd have to hide before she found out I was moving. This would be good for her. She could find a more suitable gym buddy to fill my room and cover the kitchen drawers in antibacterial contact paper like she'd always wanted. Maybe they could even share soymilk and—with a little time and a little trust—shampoo.

I got a pair of tweezers, took the peanut butter jar down from the kitchen cabinet, and started digging.

IT WAS HARD TO PIN DOWN WHICH WAS STRONGER: the desire to live like a real live grown-up or the desire to spend some quality time with the dead. True, the slutty ghosts had their appeal, but my relationship to the super-natural had a longer history than that. I was nine years old when I saw my first ghost, and I had been waiting for another ever since.

I grew up on a rarely trafficked street—the kind of street you could play just about any sport in the middle of with little automotive interruption. At night, when the occasional car passed through, I could follow its headlights as they pro-jected their way around my walls. Sometimes I'd pretend I had escaped from prison in some brilliantly confounding fashion and they were searching for me. One night when I was tucked in with my disintegrating blankie, a car passed by but failed to take the light with it. My bedroom remained dimly but steadily illuminated. I was not afraid of the dark. The dark is what happens when the sun goes down. It was like cowering from dirt. But I *was* afraid of inexplicable light. In the movies, a sudden glow was generally accompanied by exhaust fumes from an alien spaceship. It's why I was never comfortable with night-lights. They were unnatural. Plus, if they worked for me, would they not also work for the eight-eyed monster hiding in the closet? Bitch has eight eyes. She can see a night-light. Best to level the playing field.

So I crept out of my room, on the hunt for artificial brightness. I turned off the hallway light and returned to bed. *There*, I thought, *that should take care of it*. But the ghost was just getting started. The perfectly sharp silhouette of a little boy with a bowl haircut appeared in the far corner of my bedroom. He was approximately my size and shape, with a Peter Pan gait, except that he was obviously a minion of Hades. He glided across the wall, stopped, and looked up at some invisible speck on the ceiling. Then he turned to face me for a moment before quickly merging into the darkness of the adjacent wall.

And that was it. Like a photosensitive plant reaching for the sun, I widened my eyes, attempting to absorb all the paranormal presence possible. The strange cocktail of fear and magic kept my eyes bouncing from wall to wall in time with the eyes of my cat-shaped wall clock, which ticked off the seconds with its tail. I assumed the boy would cycle back, but he never did. I felt a little rejected. I always thought there was an understanding in the community of the dead that it's best to appear before children, who are more apt to accept what they're seeing. My ghost took one look at me and changed his mind.

"Hello?" I whispered. And he pretended not to hear me.

Beyond the rejection, there were pretty convincing social reasons to keep the sighting on the down low. Every nine-year-old knows the difference between wanting the impossible and getting it. I didn't need my friends shouting "Boo!" at me on the bus any more than I needed a school psychologist holding up inanimate objects and asking me if they were real. Plus, I was already starting to second-guess myself. Even if it was real, as far as paranormal experiences go, mine was pretty unsexy. Haunting Lite. It was brief and subtle and left no proof for the living—no recovered keepsakes or cardigans folded on headstones. No bones locked in a trunk in the attic, shrouded by a moth-eaten wedding veil.

So I was eager, to put it mildly, to move into McGurk's. I wanted to see what a real ghost looked like while simultaneously accessing my inner militant feminist/whore. I left a message for Sang, thanking her for showing me the apartment. When I didn't hear from her, I decided to follow up with an e-mail, thinking the chances of Sang's phone being disconnected were better than not. I felt like a desperate girl angling for a second date after my nerves had gotten the better of me on the first. Why didn't she love me? Was I not a catch? She could use my loofah if she wanted to. I never heard from her again.

It was the night before Nell reentered this half of the world. I couldn't believe I had packed in a whole real estate dalliance in the time she'd been gone. It was like the end of *The Bridges of Madison County*. The never-released director's cut of *The Bridges of Madison County*, with the dead prostitutes and the broken glass and the decapitated dolls' heads.

I sat at a bar with Mac near his new apartment, eating

stale popcorn and moping into my beer. I said I just couldn't believe Sang hadn't called.

"Who?"

"Sang."

"You did? When? You can't hold a tune."

"Shut up, racist." I laughed.

And he laughed, too. And then he stopped and said, "What are we talking about?"

For the first time, I found myself perversely grateful for Nell. If I didn't know that her punctual bill-paying and obsessive cleaning originated from a larger fissure in her psyche, I would be happy to have her as a roommate. If I lived with Mac or Sang, I might come home to find the house burned down. Mac wedged a lime into his beer and squirted himself in the face. I reminded him of his amazing apartment tip, which had turned out to be a big, fat tease, robbing me of the impossibly hip version of myself and dooming me to a life of banality and a cupboard of Snackwells sandwich cookies. Though the devil's food ones aren't half bad. Mac looked at me.

"I can honestly say I have no idea what you're talking about. Have you been smoking pot out the window again?"

"That's hardly the point."

It took a few minutes to get his version of the story. Motivated by real estate guilt, Mac confirmed, he did pass on the e-mail. That he remembered. But he claimed never to have called me beforehand, reminding me that we were only tenuously "speaking." Furthermore, the e-mail was passed on to him via a friend of a friend. He had no idea who this Sang person was.

"Why would I call you to tell you I was going to e-mail you? I'm not eighty years old."

I said I didn't know but that I had become accustomed to living with such obsessive-compulsive behavior. No amount of triple-checking or scheduling or Handi-Wiping fazed me anymore.

"I distinctly remember having this conversation with you."

"I love it!" Mac slapped the bar. "This is so like the *Twilight Zone* movie."

"That's a TV show."

"Movie."

"TV show. And are you kidding me?"

But he wasn't kidding. The more I pressed him, the further he backed away from it. My mind spun. *But Grandma's been dead for twenty years!* I had spoken to someone that night. Hadn't I? Something had stopped me from putting foam-core museum plaques next to Nell's Ansel Adams posters and sorority photos. Was it possible I had had an adulterous real estate conversation but couldn't recall with whom? Now who was the big whore? And where did this end? Maybe Sang was a ghost. She certainly had the demeanor for it. More likely, I had been a party to not one but several unaccounted-for phone calls that night. I am the thing even rarer than a ghost: a chatty pot smoker.

"This is going to drive me crazy."

"Oh, I don't know." Mac put a thumb over the neck of his beer and turned it upside down. "From where you're sitting, I think you can walk there."

INQUIRIES WERE MADE. MINOR INVESTIGATIONS launched with finesse so as not to set off any "How many fingers am I holding up?" alarms. When those proved inconclusive, it occurred to me that it didn't matter. Perhaps this is always how ghosts appear in real life. More the suggestions of themselves, a series of shadows and arrows and unaccounted-for conversations. Even if I did move downtown, I would probably never see one of McGurk's famed prostitutes in all her detailed glory. I would just see Sang, sitting barefoot at the Norwegian picnic table, one leg drawn up to her chest, staring into space. And she wouldn't be able to do that for long. . . .

Just as Nell and I had gotten back into the rhythm of things (me hiding my possessions and her hunting them down like Easter eggs), she moved out. Shortly after a new roommate moved in, I happened to walk past 295 Bowery. The building was boarded up from the inside, and a piece of official city letterhead was stuck to the door. I ducked under the orange tape and peered through a cloudy peephole. It looked the same as it had when it was inhabited. But that wasn't saying much. The only real difference was that the framed pictures were gone.

Despite valiant efforts on the part of the long-term tenants to get the building recognized as a landmark, McGurk's was evacuated and set to be torn down as soon as the city got around to it. When they did, 295 was replaced with the universally abhorred high-rise that currently bloats the space between Houston and Stanton. The building is tall and reflective, covered in futuristic (if by "future" you mean 1984) windows. They enable the residents to live on the Bowery but not live on the Bowery, to pick over choice pieces of the past and dump the rest. Don't get me wrong—I'm not one to stand on principle when I can sleep in a duplex. I wouldn't kick gentrification out of bed if it crawled in there free of charge. But it never does. And so despising it becomes not only the right thing to do but the economical thing to do. Reading the ordinance, I found some small consolation in all this, both morally and personally. My haunted real estate heaven would have quickly become a living hell. A few months of freestanding fireplaces and toothbrush haircrafting and the whole building would be dragged down into a pile of rubble. Not reduced but worse—replaced.

Already replaced was my conviction that my whole New York existence hinged on my address. Nell ceased to bother me as much once I realized how close I came to leaving her, how easy it would have been to say good-bye if Sang had welcomed me into her home with track-marked arms. I was a grown person and free to do as I pleased. It was the unhappy whores of McGurk's who were trapped at that site. I knew a thing or two about ghosts. So I knew a bulldozer, though a literal interpretation of "confronting the ghost head-on," wouldn't actually release them. Instead, they would be forced to move into the new space, fixed and displaced at the same time. They would confuse one homogeneous condominium for another. Lose one another in identical walk-in closets. Find themselves shoved into odorless rooms, where they would be doomed to run like mercury along those perfect lines where the walls meet floors for all of eternity. A horizon of happiness around every corner.

It's Always Home You Miss

Every New Yorker's personal annoyance scale is best pictured as a cell phone commercial. The semipermeable bars of varying colors and heights extend up from people's heads as they move along the sidewalk. One person finds an open-air cigar smoker more irritating than a skill-less subway performer. Another considers the person who mistakes a subway pole for a full-body pillow during rush hour exponentially worse than a taxicab keeping its overhead lights aglow despite being occupied. One person knows that frozen-yogurt chains are the devil's handiwork and will penetrate the ground levels of civilization as we know it, softening our brains into the consistency of same, like hazelnut-flavored soylent green. Another just likes low-fat dairy. You begin to wonder if all of these infractions are actually detailed in a warning pamphlet you were meant to see when you moved here. It probably had pictures of people in solid-color clothing, like those on airplane safety cards. It was slid under your front door and accidentally discarded with the take-out menus. Now you are forced to learn the rules on a case-by-case basis.

"I mean, honestly," says a speed-walking aficionado trapped behind a dawdler, "you wouldn't pull your car over in the middle of the street without signaling, would you?"

Well, no.

"And you wouldn't synchronize drive across the highway."

Certainly not!

"And you wouldn't change lanes without looking!"

Never admit you've done this.

And what of the more personal situations, the ones where money is exchanged? With so many options to get it right, people are always ready to brandish a laundry list of "no excuse" peccadilloes. No excuse for slow waiters, for faulty coffee lids, for mangled manicures—for actual bad laundry service. The question is never "Should I be annoyed?" but "How annoyed should I be?" Those cell phone bars are never not there. If you want a dead zone, move to New Mexico. But there is one annoyance common to all New Yorkers. One grain of sand slipped into every oyster, one irritant that joins us together at our intolerant edges like a giant puzzle of irritation. Local tragedies fade, scaffolding comes down, and not to worry: someone will always be there to break the buttons of your cashmere sweaters and clip their fingernails onto your lap. But some-where in that varied cacophony of callousness there is the single constant that unites us all: everyone has been victim-ized by the smell of a taxicab.

Picture it in your mind's nostril: you get in a cab in time to catch twin thugs named Vomit and Cologne assaulting a defenseless pine-tree air freshener. This is a scent that does not waft in real time so much as seeps into your memory to replace every pleasant aroma you have ever smelled with its pungency. You bury your nose in your scarf, but not before last night's Vomit throws an especially acidic right hook. Putrid as it is, you say nothing. Like a stranger on the street witnessing a lovers' quarrel, you're not sure you should interfere. But your annoyance bar is spiking. The backdraft from a cigar smoker is both avoidable with some fancy footwork and punishable with a judgmental glare. But there is no escaping the concoction of armpit and cheese rot currently molesting your face. Your mind does a quick calculation, multiplying the degree of stank by the distance between here and your destination, dividing the whole thing by your fear of overreacting. The idea that you might offend the driver is irrelevant. If he's going to tool around this town in an air bubble of poop, he should know there are consequences.

Perhaps you make a dramatic sniffing sound for effect. You think: Okay, a lover's quarrel is one thing, but when someone busts out the olfactory equivalent of nunchucks, maybe it's time to call in the authorities. Two blocks later, you demand that the cabdriver pull over, and you apologize but not sincerely. He comes slowly to a stop. Despite the fact that you can see the door handle at your side quite clearly, you fumble for it as if there's been a fire and the cab is filled with smoke. Your cabdriver notices you doing this but does not care. He doesn't know you and is thus unfamiliar with the authority of your nose or the infrequency with which you jump out of moving vehicles. It is about as likely that he will take your behavior as "constructive criticism" as it is that people working the deli will mourn the loss of your business when you storm out after waiting ten minutes to buy a six-pack of beer and a package of gummy frogs.

You glance back, checking for the next surge of oncoming traffic. The instant you're sure you won't kill yourself, you spring out the door. You do this before you can enter into a screaming match over the $2.50 minimum fare. If you can still see the location from where you hailed the cab, you don't have to pay when you get out. Everyone knows that. It's in the fine print of the gum-speckled Taxi Rider's Bill of Rights. But now what? You're still late for wherever you're going, guilty as usual of thinking the laws of time and space will bend for you because you're paying them extra to do so.

As you hail the next cab, you wonder: Did your new guy see you get out of the first? Does he think you're hostile? In possession of an explosive device? You do anything remotely off-color in this city anymore and people think you're either homeless or in possession of an explosive device. Go ahead, hover by a streetside ATM too long. Look in the window of an apartment complex that does not belong to you. Switch subway cars while the train is in motion. See what happens. There was a time when New York boasted the highest threshold for weird in the country. Between the blackout of 1977 and the closing of CBGB, you had to do a hell of a lot more than look askew at a building before someone suspected you of wanting to blow it up. Now people mourn the closing of a Starbucks on St. Marks Place and applaud the opening of an American Apparel on the Upper West Side. It's reasonable to register a noise complaint before midnight, and there's no shortage of dirty looks waiting for you if you fail to recycle whatever that is you're drinking. Our laws have become hard, our hearts soft. Of course, New York has always been the one place where people are nostalgic for when it used to be worse.

Through it all, the purpose and politics of taxis have remained constant, even if the makes and models of the vehicles have not. Even if the next car door you touch slides open like a minivan's and you wind up sitting as far away from the driver as a coffin in a hearse, the driver/passenger dynamic remains the same. It doesn't matter what your new driver thinks of you, just as it doesn't matter what you think of him. You're just a fare with hands that raise and legs that step off a curb. Taxicab drivers are like doctors. Professionals. You can't allow yourself to think they're passing judgment; otherwise, you might never go back. Often you find yourself thinking of them as your personal fleet of anonymity. Do a quick slideshow of every experience you've ever had in a cab. What if they were all the same cab? If these pleather seats could talk! The moment you shut the cab door, you can be who you want to be. If you are normally loath to make demands, you are now free to raise definitive questions: *Why this route? Can you avoid Times Square? Can you please identify this sticky substance? How in the name of all that is holy can you not smell that?* If you are a gregarious sort of person, you can finally have ten minutes of absolute silence in the presence of another human being without anyone asking you what's wrong. If you spend your day making decisions, you can stop, releasing yourself with those magic words: *Whichever way's the fastest.* Repeat it again when your driver attempts to brainstorm with you. He could tell you that the West Side Highway is closed and he'll need to swing around the moon first. *Really. Whichever way.*

You get in the new cab and sniff. You're in the clear. You say "What?" but your driver establishes that he's not addressing you by gesturing at his ear and shouting, "I'm not talking to you." When hands-free devices first began to infiltrate the cabs of New York, you found yourself annoyed by this frequent exchange, duped into making an ass out of yourself. *I am not the asshole,* you thought. If he doesn't want the Spanish Inquisition, maybe he should keep his voice down. But these days this banter only makes you feel stupid. By now you should really know better. And *of course* he's not talking to you. It must take a lot of restraint on the cabdriver's part not to whip around and say, "Why, do you speak Punjabi?" You marvel at the round-the-clock friend-ships and strong familial ties cabdrivers must maintain. You can barely stand to talk on the phone with friends anymore. Mostly because you can never figure out how to end con-versations without apologizing for ending them. This goes double for blood relations. To get your taxi license in New York, you must be a phone person first and a person who stops at red lights second. A very distant second.

Your next order of business is to smack the off button on the increasingly ubiquitous taxicab TVs. You must do this before one of the female talking heads can take you to a new karaoke bar or make you wait with her for Shakespeare in the Park tickets. Or put on a sexy apron behind the scenes of a famous restaurant. Shield your eyes from this bizarre display of false modesty and kitchen knives.

No, you hold the knife by the handle.

Wait, let me get my hair out of my face. Okay, like this?

No, that's the blade, and now you're bleeding everywhere.

Darn it!

Maybe if you hit the screen hard enough, you'll get lucky and break it. Try not to think about how many greasy pointer fingers have touched that exact same spot. The idea of the taxicab TV turns every New Yorker into an erratically gesticulating Woody Allen.

"What do you need TV for? You've got the best slide-show in the world!" says you-slash-Woody.

"I like it," says the tourist. "It makes the time go by faster."

"You couldn't do that at home? Who goes on vacation to make it go by faster? Would it kill you to stop and smell the urine?"

"There's nothing to take pictures of in here."

"Get out," says you-slash-Woody.

You try to imagine exactly for whom these mini movie reviews and weather reports are meant. Often even the tourists find them repugnant. Most foreigners are already so disgusted by the garish hue of our cabs that there's no point in speculating about their reaction to an all-you-can-eat dim sum festival streaming in their faces as they are held hostage by the vehicle of laziness that made us fat to begin with. They do not share our disgust so much as mock its insufficiency.

Now that you've blackened the box, you're free to turn your focus outward. Roll down the window for the occasional breeze that kicks up when the traffic lights go green. As you rush past the sidewalks of downtown, you wonder why it is that you never see anyone you know from a cab. You rarely leave the house without bumping into someone on foot. Often you're doing something very unappealing because you've become unconsciously dependent on strangers accepting and veering from your craziness. You should probably just learn to pull yourself together. Take care of that in the bathroom. Make eye contact with a mirror before you leave the house. Because how many times have you been caught in the presence of a coworker or a former lover, forced to explain away your picking and spilling and muttering? Where do these people hide when you are prepared for them? Who are these new faces waiting for the walk sign to change? Is there a formula to it? Speed + blocks covered ÷ weather = less awkward interaction. Or is it just one of the city's little mysteries, like how no one has ever seen a baby pigeon? Maybe you just don't have that many friends. That's probably it.

Suddenly, you feel exhausted, thinking about your life. All this taking stock can take a higher toll than a trip to the airport. You look up at the lights of the hotels in Midtown and wonder if you shouldn't just check into one of them. Tell the cab to stop right here, stop paying rent, crush your cell phone, deplete your bank account, stare at the wallpaper. Do not, by any means, check into the Pierre or one of the boutique hotels downtown. Staying in a great hotel when you're happy is wonderful. Staying in one when you've worked yourself up into a taxicab depression feels fatal. The good news is, it's started to rain. Pedestrians are putting their palms up to measure droplet frequency and reaching for the black umbrellas they just left in restaurant booths.

Since you're already cocooned in your banana chariot, you indulge in a little schadenfreude—the ultimate New York comfort food, surpassing even the cupcake.

The bad news is, now you're trapped in traffic. There will be no keeping the frustration at bay when you look at your watch and realize that terrible truth: the subway would have been faster. Once this occurs to you, it cannot unoccur to you. You delve deeper into the fantasy of punctuality, speculating about what stop you'd be at right now. Underground You always moves faster than Aboveground You. Underground You always arrives at the platform just as the train's pulling in and never has to contend with crowded stairs or construction delays. Force yourself to imagine the more realistic alternative. The one that has the would-be passengers, jostling and anxious, leaning into the dark tunnel. They're hoping for a glimpse of a moving light, triple-checking to make sure the illumination in the tunnel is attached to a wall and not a front car. They look like synchronized pink flamingos—one leg up, leaning out with their long necks.

It's not working. You know in your heart you'd have been there by now. Your driver starts openmouthed munching on potato chips or Cheez Doodles and you burrow a Care Bear Stare into the back of his head. You think: There are a finite number of nacho cheese Doritos in this world. He has to run out eventually. He doesn't.

"This is good," you say, a full block from your destination.

You're no physics expert, but at the speed your driver has been going, there's no way he can come to a full stop on command without killing you both. He taps the meter to make it stop. He faces forward, making eye contact only during the exchange of paper, the proof of your time together. You see his eyes in the rearview mirror. No matter how you pay—cash or credit, with a request for the overhead reading light or a request for a receipt—he looks vaguely disappointed in you.

You're out of the cab, but you're not done yet. Chances are, much like the Vomit that stank up your first cab, you're going to have to come back out the way you came. Hours later, you step onto the street and walk up a block to the next major avenue. You raise your hand to hail a cab. You leave it up there, regardless of spotting available cabs. It's a strangely lazy gesture, based on muscle memory more than effort. The rain has stopped, but it's dark outside now. If you're not drunk, you're tired, and if you're not tired, you should be. It's been a long day. But there is good news. The Fates reward you instantly. The next wave of cars includes one with a bright light on top, like a glowing fez. It veers seamlessly toward you, having mastered the art of whisking. Inside, the cab is odor-free and clean. Or at least clean enough that nothing reflects or sticks or moves in the dark.

You provide your home address, turn the TV off with your knuckle, and settle in for some AM radio and irresponsible texting. But don't get too comfortable.

Around this time, the driver blows straight past your street. It's after midnight on a school night. Sure, there's a possibility this is one of those nights where you're ready for round two, perhaps off to a secret bar or illegal gambling club or something too fantastic for words. In those cases, you might have provided an incorrect address. But tonight chances are you're going home. This is the new, more whole-some New York, after all. Most everyone's going home. When you point this out, your driver ardently insists that you gave him the wrong address all those many traffic lights ago. You are annoyed, bars above your head spiking. You may not know much, but, like a kindergartner, you know where you live. The seconds feel alive as you move farther away from your actual destination. Why, you wonder, is it always home they miss? In the daylight, when you're late to some activity you'd just as soon skip, they practically mem-orize the floor and suite number. Practically drive you up the side of the building. But when all you want to do is curl up so that you can start afresh tomorrow, you find yourself on an unsolicited tour of your own neighborhood. So you say something nonsensical, like "Why would I have gotten my own address wrong?"

Don't do that.

You're right, of course. But there's no way you're going

to win this argument. All he needs is an excuse to yell at you. He doesn't know you. He's seen one hundred other people today just like you. What he knows is this city. He is what keeps it in motion. He is the roller ball. The way you think of taxis, he thinks of people. He hears the slamming of doors, the losing of stray things, the charming beginnings and frustrating endings of relationships, our worst selves and our best. We are a blur of sliding butts and straddling legs and leaning elbows. Of "Can I smoke in here?" and "Can I get five dollars back?" All set to the soundtrack of receipts sputtering out from the taxi hull in a million tiny waves, breaking over every borough, white curls crashing down at the edges of a concrete and canary-colored ocean. And his hearing, like your sense of smell, is impeccable.

Light Pollution

W hy not just call it shit?"

I have been staring out the window at a blur of wildflowers, and this is the first sentence to leave my mouth in forty-five minutes. A high-speed conveyor belt of daisies and Arctic violets is pulled through my field of vision as we zip along a desolate Alaskan road. In the backseat of an SUV headed south on the Kenai Peninsula, I am as much out of place inside the car as outside of it. A seven-year inhabitant of Manhattan, I am woefully unfamiliar with what the rest of the country drives. It's difficult to be in any vehicle without staring suspiciously at the dashboard, keeping an eye on a meter that's not there. Like a limb long since blown off in some unnamed war, but which I persist in scratching. No one in Alaska notices me doing this, and they wouldn't— inhabitants of the "Lower 48" are notoriously suspicious and amusingly paranoid, mistaking mountains for glaciers and asking dumb questions about avalanche triggers. Why should my reaction to a family-sized vehicle be any different? They're probably amazed I didn't try to lick the tires or get in through the windows. I'm a little amazed myself.

The only reason I even know I'm in an SUV is because when I retell this story to friends back home in the weeks that follow, I describe the vehicle as "like a van but nice."

My friend April, in the passenger seat, twists around.

"Why not just call what 'shit'?"

"Bear poop." I giggle, pushing forward into the gap between the front seats.

I am more like a child in Alaska than I have been in years. Probably more like a child than when I was a child. Everything here is new and tremendous, and this feels like vacating in a way all other vacations have not. Not only am I physically dwarfed by the scenery, but going to Alaska seems like something my family would have done in the '80s but never did. Do people fly across the country just to see it anymore? To tour the homes where presidents were born? Do they go to the zoo and buy plastic visors? Make pilgrimages to houses made entirely of corn? They should. American appreciation vacations have become the purview of the very local or the very foreign. Which is a shame. The song doesn't go "If you can't be with the one you love, leave the country."

But back to the poop. After a hike in the woods outside Anchorage, I have learned that bear feces is called "scat."

Actually, "woods" is a bit of a misnomer. The strip of trees in my parents' backyard, that sacred burial ground for our pets, is "wooded." The voodoo-stick-doll-sprinkled camping grounds of *The Blair Witch Project* are located "in the woods." I, on the other hand, was tripping on the root structures of spruce trees taller than my apartment building back home, trying to avoid poisonous plants the size of my toilet.

That's where I spotted the sign that (a) taught me my new word for the day and (b) warned me against "engaging a bear," should I cross one's path. Since the latter bit of information was easily dismissed (I get it: the bear wins; I'm not going to ask it to play poker), I chose to focus on the scatological. At the time I did not make the connection between the adjective for "prevalence of shit" and its abbreviation in noun form. Perhaps this is because, for longer than I care to admit, I thought "scatological" was an adjective for "all over the place." On countless occasions, I had accused other people of being "scatological," meaning "mercurial; please try to focus." When in fact I was accusing them of being full of shit. This explained a lot. And if you believe something for a long enough time, it's hard to replace that belief, even if you know it's wrong.

"I think it's because it's not just feces," says Jeff, my friend's fiancé, in the driver's seat. "It has something to do with the percentage of the shit that's actually in scat. There's fur in there. Other fur."

But of course. *Other fur*. Why not? Only a few days in and nothing surprises me about Alaska. It is a land of casual extremes, a place located not only on the fringes of the planet but on the fringes of all normalcy. A place where you could wake up one morning to a caribou giving birth in your back-yard and you'd go to work anyway. You're not even sure where your camera is. Life is both worshipped and expend-able in equal doses. And the human population is as serious as the scenery.

Here is a list of the six types of Alaskan residents, not including native tribes:

1. Military personnel
2. State-builders
3. Nature enthusiasts (by which I mean raw, in-your-face nature; bird-watching is for house cats)
4. Hippie nutballs who looked at Portland, Oregon, and thought, *This is way too urban; I have to get out of here.*
5. People who have at one point done something very illegal involving a sawed-off shotgun and freezer bags
6. This guy:

When I boarded my flight to Anchorage in Chicago, I went to wedge my trashy magazines into the polyester pouch in front of me. There was something more substantial than usual in there between the SkyMall catalog and the safety card. It was a library book. I was intrigued. It was like finding an abandoned toy in a random bathroom stall, but less creepy. I let the pocket snap shut before opening it again. On the spine in big, bold letters, it read: *The Amityville Horror: A True Story*. Nope, just as creepy.

Passengers were still streaming down the aisle, clutching their boarding passes and looking above the seats, as if trying to remember the alphabet. I quickly shoved the book into the pouch to my right and tried to forget about it. My seatmate turned out to be a state-builder Alaskan. His grandfather had a small bay named after him. He was on his way home to visit his mother, who made custom shotgun cases.

"She does *not*."

"Well, no"—he looked at me thoughtfully—"she doesn't make the cases themselves, but you should see what she does with them."

I imagined this man's mother in a floral muumuu, beating the shit out of a sea otter on the front porch.

Apparently, what she actually does is decorate the cases. Causing no small amount of pride in her son, she was recently commissioned to make one for a Jerry Falwell–like figure I should have heard of but hadn't. At the base, she Krazy Glued a bleeding crucifix of red rhinestones and her logo: *A Case of Class by Melina*. He handed me her card.

"I'm Earl," he said, stiffly shaking my hand in such close proximity to his chest, it gave the illusion of palsy.

"Sloane." I shook back, trying on the the-less-you-talk-the-harder-you-are theory of man-speak.

"This your first time going to Alaska?"

"It is."

"Well, she's a beauty."

"Is she prettier than a boat?"

Earl opened his pouch, took one look at *The Amityville Horror*, shrugged, and saw it as a repository for chewing gum.

"Prettier. But she has a dark side. Weird stuff goes down. I don't think people think of Alaska like that."

"That's more or less exactly how they think of it," I said, and proceeded to index every ax murder I knew of on my fingers.

"So, Earl, you can see how the stories become geographically dense and objectively creepier as you move farther north and west."

"I guess so." He frowned thoughtfully. "Now that you mention it . . ."

Earl proceeded to tell me about a murder case in which a bakery owner was making brioche by day and picking up strippers at a club near the airport by night. This particular baker charmed the strippers into his prop plane and took them to one of the many secluded islands off Alaska's coast. Once on the island, the man's demeanor changed dramatically. He forced the strippers to get completely naked, pulled out a crossbow, and informed them that they had twenty minutes to hide, at which point he was going to hunt them down and kill them. As sure as the dough rises, that's what he did. This man turned from baker to butcher, murdering about twenty girls in this way.

To be naked ever in Alaska is already to be inconvenienced. The place is exactly as cold as you think it is. But the most shocking part of the story was that the teller *knew* the subject. Earl and his mother and his mother's BeDazzler lived down the road from him. On his way to his old logging job, Earl would get a coffee and bear claw (almond, not keratin) from him.

"He made the best jelly doughnuts I've ever tasted," Earl said, in complete and total seriousness.

TOMORROW IS THE WEDDING OF JEFF, THE driver of our vehicle, and my dear friend April, the shotgun holder. Here I am referring to the term for the front seat of a car. I think we can all agree this warrants clarification, having nothing to do with killing sprees or unplanned pregnancies. The event has all the trappings of a destination wedding—jet lag, group hikes, a plane ticket for which I could exchange a month's rent—but in fact, our little community of tourists is small. One hundred twenty out of the one hundred twenty-five guests are native Alaskans. I am one of the other five, a member of the bridal party. We are a nervous band of outsiders. We are quick to highlight our own ignorance, blurting out things like "I don't know how to play ice hockey!" when someone casually points to a pond. We think if we surrender our pride early, the state will have mercy on us. The paranoia about wildlife is, frankly, a whole other animal. See: *Is that a wolf? I thought I just saw a wolf. Oh, wait, that's a dog. And it's not moving. I think that's a lawn dog.*

Because Canada, the Great White North, is a very dark place, when our plane descended through the clouds, it was like landing in a secret city. I had the same feeling the first time I flew to England. After hours of ocean, I experienced an awe at the reality of the world. To have so much nothing and then something: when you are a novice traveler, London feels like Papua New Guinea. Compounding this sensation in Anchorage was the fact that the only regular pollution is light pollution. Though "pollution" is a little harsh. Anchorage at night is "movie dark," a perpetual dusk in which the cameras have to capture the actors' faces even though it's supposed to be midnight.

For the first time I understood why people come back from Alaska with fifty pictures of glaciers or return from a honeymoon in Tahiti with fifty pictures of the same sunset. The world is so beautiful in these places, it is impossible to

register that there will be more, more, more. Surely this is
it. Negotiate with your ailing camera battery. How can it not
stay alive for this? How can you believe that twenty minutes from now there will be an even *taller* forest, an even
wider waterfall? We are only as good as our most extreme
experiences.

WHEN THE BRIDAL PARTY ARRIVED, WE WERE LESS
of a "party" and more of a bunch of separate people flying
in from different locations. Still, April insisted on making
trip after trip to retrieve us from the airport, scoffing at the
idea of taxi services. This gesture seemed saintly by New
York standards. Until I realized that it's generally warmer
in one's car than anywhere else and there is no real traffic
in Anchorage. Even if there was, I wouldn't have minded
waiting. The Anchorage airport is a pleasant place to visit.
While you can't eat off the floor, you can drop your scarf
on it without hesitating to wrap it back around your neck.
Which is more than I can say for JFK. Plus, the Anchorage airport has a gift shop called "Moosellaneous." And a
fiber-optic starry night on the baggage-claim ceiling, which
one finds particularly hypnotic after a long flight. As I came
down one of the escalators, there was a person in a polar-
bear plushy suit, wearing a Native American headdress on

top and handing out flyers. As he wordlessly pointed me toward the exit, I thought, *Where is David Lynch when you need him?*

I was the last to arrive. When April and I walked through her front door, there were clear signs that merriment had gone on without me. Around her condo were scattered open greeting cards with miniature lace dresses glued to the covers, stained wineglasses, and slicks of soft cheese on a plate in the sink. Everyone was asleep, and all the beds were claimed. April showed me to my room, a cot in the laundry room with a sleeping bag unfurled on top. She reemerged with a second sleeping bag.

"Oh, I already have one." I pointed to the cot.

"I know." She also pointed to the cot.

A frigid blast came through a crack in the window and knocked the paper brides on their faces.

IT IS THE NEXT MORNING, AND JEFF HAS GRA-ciously agreed to spend his last day of bachelordom driving his fiancée and five of her girlfriends down the coast. Part of me thinks this is the least he can do, as all of us have flown past Canada to get here. This is a common observation among our group, a default fascination triggered by the sight of one's breath or the glare of the sun at night: *Dude, we're above* Canada.

The state of Alaska itself is like one big whale. Chunks of ice the size of Rhode Island exist like barnacles. They could detach from a glacier up north and no one would notice. During my time there, no fewer than three people explained to me that if you took the outline of Alaska and superimposed it over the continental United States, it would stretch across the country end to end. They must teach this in elementary school up there, because it had the same delivery I like to employ for "Well, you know, yellow's a primary color" and "A tomato is actually a fruit." It makes sense to imagine Alaska in this way, as a giant sheet of shadow pulled over our cities and hills. It is a dwarfing place. It manages to be both roughly lumbering and quietly graceful, light about twenty hours a day but dark on the ground. Every mountain passed is so imposing, it would be *the* mountain if transplanted south. What I see from across a gas station on a dirt road would be the main attraction in, I don't know, Missouri. As we drive, the combination of soaring mountains and low clouds gives the illusion of smoke—of a series of forest fires. So much so that the sight of each mountain sets off a small panic in my chest until I grow accustomed to the view.

In a less tangible way, I feel I am in Alaska at a very fragile time. I arrived at the Ted Stevens airport one week after the senator had been ousted from office for accepting illegal campaign donations. Now I insist on tooling around the town of Girdwood as if I have a crush on Ted Stevens.

I am looking for his house, which was built with the blood of baby caribou. Or just dirty money. Meanwhile, banners line the paved streets of Anchorage, announcing that the following year is the state's fiftieth anniversary. I feel the way the Italians and Chinese must feel when we point to the Liberty Bell and say, "Look at this old thing we built. We are pleased with it."

At one point, April's mother notes that there is something in the air these days besides the usual (just more air). In addition to the mysteriously high number of bear attacks this summer, there are rumors that Alaska's otherwise unknown governor is on the short list for the Republican vice presidential ticket. She refers to this woman as "our Sarah Palin," which strikes me as pleasantly loyal. *Our Sarah Palin.* Perhaps it reveals a political passivity on my part, but I don't think of any of New York's politicians as mine. Not in the "Our little Mikey's all grown up" way. Then again, I wouldn't elect a child to office, and perhaps that's the way it should be. Their feet flail around when they sit, and they have a tendency to stick gum underneath the desks.

Palin's nomination will serve as a strange social call to arms among the Alaskans I know living in New York, like the way one twin can sometimes feel the pain of another from miles away. Except, in this case, one of the twins considers the other an embarrassment, the worst Alaskan PR tragedy since Jewel started publishing poetry or—as even

Earl put it—"the time that moron walked into the woods to die in a bus." Each time Palin winks at the world, one of my Alaskan friends feels a deep pang of shame. But like the rest of the country, right now I know absolutely nothing about Sarah Palin. For now I think, *Good for Sarah Palin! Good for April's mom! Good for Alaska!* Politicians are like Olympians. Every four years they bloom into the American consciousness, but they've been there this whole time, putting down roots beneath the surface. I am excited for this sneak preview of what's to come. I look forward to parties back in New York in which I will know a thing or two about contemporary politics.

"And there"—Jeff ducks forward a little and points—"is where we used to camp and fish when we were little."

I scan the solid patch of spruce trees to which Jeff has gestured. I look for a path or even a gap in the foliage. Starting from the sky, there's a layer of light blue, then a layer of white, then a layer of green, and then a layer of dirt. If the Alaskan state flag were striped instead of starred, these would be the colors, and this would be the order.

"But"—Jeff's voice trails off—"you can see how overrun it's become."

My heart goes out to Jeff. To the naked eye, he is far more out of place on this road trip than I am. He is our lone star of testosterone in a galaxy of chick. I spend much of the car ride wheeling through my iPod, on the hunt for songs that don't instantly conjure footage of hipster girls ironically sipping Pabst with their cheeks sucked in. I must have music that corresponds with the dead-serious consumption of Pabst. Even a band called Grizzly Bear feels too tame. Jeff is millionth-generation state-builder Alaskan. His family helped create the state—specifically, the railroads—which connected oil towns to fishing towns, and fishing towns to gold-rush towns, and so forth. This fascinates me in a way that does not fascinate Jeff himself. He is used to his own background, even used to outsiders' interest in it. Absolutely no one will ever say to me, *No way, you grew up in suburbia? Man, that must have been amazing.*

I MET APRIL WHEN SHE WAS SPENDING HER POST-graduate years in New York, where I was spending mine as well. April was raised in a city where the fog has been known to freeze and fall on people's heads. A city where the swank downtown neighborhood is dubbed SoNo (South of Nordstrom). For a place with so much clean air, it was strangely suffocating. She was ready for something a bit more fast-paced in SoCa (South of Canada). New York was her first choice. We exchanged a few sideways glances during a health-care-benefits orientation at work. Then we went around the conference table sharing arbitrary facts about ourselves. I divulged that I had never been stung by a bee. April said she was from Alaska.

"Alaska!" The human resources lady brightened. "Hey, now! I'm sure New York will seem like Jamaica to you."

April gritted her teeth and let out a fake laugh, the kind where one pronounces the word "ha." The assumption of dramatic regional evolution is one of humanity's odder tics. I, for example, do not listen to every schizophrenic hobo muttering to himself on the subway or cover my ears when the train comes. But must I be diagnosed by the rest of the country as legally deaf? How many times has it been suggested that I will actually have difficulty falling asleep in someone's peaceful country house? People of central Africa, I beg you: never come here unless you are willing to sit in a locked sauna and have some bozo say the words "I'll bet this feels like air-conditioning to you."

"It's a little infuriating," admitted April, as we sat on the metal benches of a corporate office park and ate salad-bar lunches.

"It's like they want to take away my socks and dunk me in ice water. I never realized how little people knew about Alaska."

Perhaps to appear more knowledgeable than the human-resources lady, I told April the only thing I knew about Alaska. It was an old news story about some local Anchorage kids who decided to sneak into the zoo's polar-bear exhibit and swim across the moat. Alaska may have a free-for-all Noah's-ark quality when it comes to breeds of puffin, but a polar bear is a big deal. Those they lock up. The tragedy was amplified each time I heard it. In one version, one of the kids was being mauled and crying for help as the other two jumped back in the moat. Sometimes only one of the boys swam back. Sometimes none of them swam back. Sometimes they were all found dead, floating in the red water. It took on the quality of a morality play, awkwardly undercut with Darwinian themes of stupidity.

April rested her plastic fork in her salad bowl and, in the same tone Earl would employ when discussing jelly doughnuts years later, said, "I had homeroom with those boys."

"Oh my God."

"No"—she put her hand on my knee—"I'm kidding."

"Oh, phew."

"Actually"—she laughed—"I'm not. But I wanted to get that worried look off your face."

We quickly made the transition from amicable coworkers to voluntary friends. Eventually we moved a building away from each other on the same block in Manhattan. It was like a Broadway musical, if only in set design. Our apartments faced the same inaccessible courtyard, and a typical phone conversation might go something like this:

APRIL: Hey, it's me. Do you smell that?

ME: No, smell what?

APRIL: Walk over to your back window. I think something's burning.

ME: I think . . . Yes, that's definitely barbecue.
APRIL: Good, just checking.

Most people have at least one friend in New York who never gives up the crusade to make their lives feel rural, and April was mine. Assuming you're not one of those "no furniture, no hot water, no problem" people, we all have elements of self-comfort in the beginning. Means of making our lives feel a bit more civilized. But gradually the city fights back, like crabgrass. Not that you know what crabgrass looks like anymore. You stop setting your alarm clock early and start vowing to run only when chased. You make peace with those cracks and corners of your apartment that came ground to the floorboards with rust and dirt. You tack up articles about museum exhibits, only to tear them down months later when you realize the show has moved to Moscow. The diligent sheen wears off your book club until it's more of a wine club until it's not even in someone's apartment anymore until it's just drinks and a movie and enough last-minute cancellation e-mails to, ironically, fill a book.

But April really went to the museums and the book clubs and the black-and-white movies in the park. She painted her walls, stripped her floors, and drilled nails into the exposed brick. From these she hung matted photos of Alaska so green you got the sense the air quality was better in the space around the frame. Photos that looked like they were shot for the very purpose of selling picture frames. Whose mountains are so lush? Whose nieces so perfect and healthy? Perhaps those related to a woman who would regularly go into bodegas and inquire about the freshness of the clementines on display outside.

She read in *Time Out New York* that it was possible to go down to a pier in Chelsea and go kayaking in the Hudson. As if this weren't miraculous enough, she actually succeeded in getting me to do this with her. With the caveat that she would inoculate me with Purell beforehand and pay for a Turkish masseuse to scrub me down with steel wool if we capsized. While I eyed the slick rainbow bubbles on the water's surface, she let her paddle rest on her lap and tilted her face up toward the sun. When she opened her eyes again, she said, "How much further do you think we can paddle out?"

The time we drove upstate to visit the small, artsy town of Beacon, she seemed disappointed that it only took two hours to get there. She had rented a jeep. We ate French onion soup at a diner with cake plates on the counter. As we cleaned the cheese from the side of the bowl with our fingers, I asked April if there was anything she didn't love about this Alaska of hers. She thought for a while. She was dismissive of Juneau and Fairbanks. She mentioned the people there wearing Carhartts all year round. When I said, "What are Carhartts?" I was told with exasperation, "They're *very* Fairbanks."

As the day wound down, we ducked in and out of the crafts and antiques shops of the rainy Rockwellesque streets. April picked out a set of hand-painted mugs.

"Look at this one." She held a yellow striped mug by its handle. A three-dimensional porcelain bee stuck to the rim.

"When are you going to use *that* in real life?"

"I just installed mug hooks in my kitchen," she replied, as if it were the most obvious answer in the world.

"And"—she sidled up to the antique cash register—"this is real life."

I was distraught when she moved back home, though my sadness was tempered by the shipping rates to Alaska that resulted in her unloading half her worldly possessions onto me. Among other things, I became the proud owner of three "decorative" ledges, a set of ice-cream bowls, and two egg coddlers—everyday objects that I couldn't conceive being a part of my every day but that made me miss April each time I ate lo mein out of the ice-cream bowls or used the egg coddlers for bourbon.

It was only six years later, as I arrived in Alaska just past midnight, that I understood how strange it was for her to be in New York in the first place. If you're lucky enough to become truly close with a stranger in New York, there will still be a part of you and a part of them that's reduced to novelty. You can know everything about them, every detail of their childhood—every name of every hamster—and there will always be something that you can't help but view as an accessory. It's difficult to parse out someone else's formative moments from their trivial ones when you weren't there to witness either. April's being from Alaska was no different from her being my adopted friend or my actress friend or my friend who fact-checked at a magazine by day and stripped at Scores by night. Her Alaskanness was the piece of her framed on the wall. A point of entry taken for granted, no more a part of the room than the door frame.

IN THE WEEKS BEFORE WE LEFT FOR THE WEDDING, the other members of the bridal party, now securely fastened in their heated SUV bucket seats, displayed the same level of casual awe and anticipation regarding our trip to the top of the planet. E-mail chains wound back and forth. *This time next week, we'll be in Anchorage: can you believe it!?* I couldn't. Alaska felt like a slightly exaggerated trip to the Northwest on one hand, and like Pluto, that forlornly demoted planet, on the other.

As I laid out my long underwear, I took my globe down from a bookshelf and sat on my floor with my legs stretched out. It is a world in which one can still book a flight to Yugoslavia. A world in which there is a dotted line that curves down Germany in semi-fetal position, dividing it into East and West. I imagine the boardroom discussion about the

globe, the now dated debate as to how to represent the Berlin Wall.

> GLOBE GUY #1: Let's look at the Great Wall of China.
> What'd we do there?
>
> GLOBE GUY # 2: That's not a border.
>
> GLOBE GUY #1: Well, we can't go around just doling
> out lines. If tomorrow I make a bay out of banana
> peels, do I get to have an estuary? No, I don't.
>
> GLOBE GUY #2: But you can't cross the wall with-
> out getting shot or paying someone not to shoot
> you. So, by the Mexican definition, they should get
> a line.
>
> GLOBE GUY #1: You're fired.
>
> GLOBE GUY #3 (*leaning on a stack of atlases in the corner,*
> *sporting a watch fob; he lights a cigarette*): You could
> always make it . . . dotted.
>
> *Silence all around.*
>
> GLOBE GUY #2: You know you can't smoke in here.

I rotated the globe east, my finger fixed on the latitude at
the crown of the world. Printed in eight-point type were the
dates explorers first set snowshoe on the North Pole. Except,
because it's my globe we're talking about, the paper had been
scratched away, and instead of reading *Reached North Pole*,
it says *ached North*. I found this so amusing, I immediately

e-mailed it to the one other bridesmaid who refers to Central Park as "the woods."

She responded: *That's hilarious! Are you bringing your own waders? Because I've been looking online and I think it might be unhygienic to rent them.*

But now, one week and four thousand miles later, it appears I have been duped into false camaraderie. I know these women call the urban centers of the Lower 48 "home." I've witnessed some of them order brunch as if they're competing to see whose food gets spat in first. But apparently they have also been camping in northern Michigan and skiing in Colorado. Voluntarily. All of a sudden it turns out they spent their childhoods spotting coyotes outside Jackson Hole or hiking the Appalachian Trail. I begin to suspect we share a different definition of "amateur" when it comes to the greatest of great outdoors. As they select fly-fishing rods without hesitation and brandish Clif bars at the slightest stomach growl, I realize these women are not kindred. They are nature's pool sharks. A few days on a glorified Outward Bound excursion, and out come the hourly declarations of their need for fresh air, reveries of piney appreciation and mountain worship that peak with vows to chuck their mainland lives and move to Alaska at once. They are up for everything and I am down for the count, slipping on some rocks and falling ass-first into the Russian River wearing head-to-toe fleece. They have cameras with multiple lenses and a base tan of outdoorsy-ness that prevents them from asking inane questions about why ice melts. Whereas I am bright red with ignorance, my dilettante skin verbally peeling in the backseat with each mispronounced inlet.

This could be part of a larger problem. If there is a line finer than my globe's tiny stream of German dots, it is the line between acclimation and simulation. Between participation and sublimation. Basically: what's being a good sport and what's the plot of a bad romantic comedy? City gals don't trek up glaciers in designer heels any more than country folk wander down dark alleys to ask gangbangers for directions. People tend to be more tofu-like, able to absorb whatever environment they're dropped into. But where does the adaptability end and your actual personality begin? At the rehearsal dinner, someone will tell me I bear a striking resemblance to the Inputs, the only Inuit tribe legally allowed to hunt whale. I will be disproportionately flattered by this information, and intrigued by the possibility of decreasing my Con Ed bill by heating my apartment with blubber. I have what it takes to be part of the Alaskan fabric. But that doesn't mean I'm about to go out and harpoon a humpback.

I AM SATISFIED WITH JEFF'S DEFINITION OF "SCAT," as it feels like what I have come to refer to as Alaskan Logic. That is, something so fundamental it never occurred to me. If you'd like to be reminded of your mortality, go into any drugstore around Juneau. Next to the deodorant and the toothpaste are packages of windproof matches and water-purifying tablets. The "welcome basket" in our cabin included a bag of granola, socks, trail maps, and a giant bell labeled "bear bell." I thought this was a joke. Just the way "seal be gone" spray or "anti-puffin" darts might have been a joke. But later, when April sat us down by the roaring fireplace in the middle of August and doled out a pre-hike lecture on bear safety, the bell seemed just a bit less funny.

I had a flash of April's expression back in New York when I relayed my distilled version of the polar bear story. A moat full of teenage-boy blood swirled around in my imagination.

As recently as last week and as close as a mile away, a woman was on her front porch and was mauled by a bear. She had startled the bear by leaning down to pick a flower. She was without a bell. The fact that she was reaching not for a half-used cigarette butt but for a flower—one of God's little sprinkles!—made the story exponentially worse. Unlike the legend of the polar bears, this one was far more real. Perhaps it's just because I'm not a big swimmer, but I do like to pick a nice wildflower.

The other women dispersed to their neatly organized canvas totes and quilted duffel bags. A tinny chime set off as each bell made contact with its owner. I stood there, smiling into the middle distance between me and the fire, trying to recall if I had kept the bear bell or if I threw it away with the gift wrapping. April waved her hand to unglaze my face.

"Sloane."

"Yes? Present."

"Do you have your bear bell?"

"Yes."

"Do you want to go get it?"

"Get what?"

"The bear bell."

"Get the bear bell?"

"Yes, get the bear bell."

"Sure, I'll go get the bear bell."

I ransack my luggage, removing most of the items from my suitcase until it is light enough for me to lift and shake. I listen closely, as if it were an enormous cell phone. I am filled with gratitude when I hear a faint ringing in one of the outside pockets. Clap if you believe in keeping your limbs, Tink! When I return to the fire, everyone is already at the bottom of the driveway, packing themselves into a big van. Most have their hair in high ponytails, with their respective bells tucked into their swinging manes.

Usually I am hesitant about wearing my hair in a high ponytail. I didn't cheerlead for a reason. Also, I once heard that rapists prey on women with ponytails, pulling them like handles. But now that my pinnacle danger has been transferred to getting *scalped by a fucking bear*, I am only too quick to loop the ribbon around the tight elastic. I join the chorus of chiming initiated by every sharp turn the SUV takes. Safety first.

It's ten-thirty p.m., and the sun is finally beginning to set. The sun itself isn't directly visible from the backseat, but its presence is acknowledged by the snowcaps on each peak. These turn a deep pink when the clouds break above them. Jeff lowers his visor to avoid direct eye contact with the sudden flashes of light that bounce off the road. Meanwhile, the rivers we pass are an incongruously bright tropical blue, largely because they are not rivers. They are glacial runoffs, surging with the purest water on the planet. Alaska is what happens when Willy Wonka and the witch from Hansel and Gretel elope, buy a place together upstate, renounce their sweet teeth, and turn into health fanatics. The gutters swell with spring water. The streets are paved with Swiss chard.

As we round a bend in the road, we come upon a field of my favorite and only distinctly *unhealthy* Alaskan specialty, the Ghost Forest. In the past week, I have seen twelve sea lions, four otters, three moose, one bald eagle, and a crazed puffin with a seagull vendetta. But nothing reminds me I'm in Alaska like the Ghost Forests.

"Those are freaky-looking," says one of the bridesmaids in dismissive disgust. As a policy, she oohs and aahs only at things with paws. Maybe I should get out of the car and slap some oven mitts on the branches.

But she's right. They are freaky-looking. In 1964, a massive 9.2 earthquake devastated southcentral Alaska. It was by far the most powerful in U.S. history, and one of the largest recorded of all time. It created a lethal tsunami that reached as far as the Hawaiian islands and pinballed between them. Back in Alaska, there were aftershocks—disguised as 6.0 full-blown earthquakes—for an entire year. I imagine the Alaskan terrain itself looking down at California and thinking, *My earthquake eats your earthquake for breakfast.* When the plates shifted, the land not only cracked but actually dropped toward the earth's core. This happened so quickly that the root systems of whole forests were exposed, flooded, and destroyed. But the wood itself was preserved from the inside out by salt water. Refusing to rot like normal dead trees, the Ghost Forests remain to this day, the wet dream of Edward Gorey's landscape architect. They are vegetative vampires—so pale they glow at night, branches sharp like fangs, not dead but frozen. As the car speeds along, I try to pick out one tree from the blur on which to focus, following it from the front of the window to the back.

That's when it happens.

My seat belt tears tight across my chest. My stomach lurches, gravitating toward my lungs. My neck bends forward and returns upright. The car swerves and the tires screech and I hear Jeff scream, "Oh, shit! Oh, shit!" with unmitigated panic. Thoughts are corralled into half-seconds. My head is on fire, my synapses cast in the role of hero and trying to get every image out of the back of my mind and up front to safety. I wonder if we are careening off a cliff. I think, *No, it's August—what's there to glide on? Are we even on a cliff?* I see ice. People can career off ice. Am I going to die like this? Will I drown? And is that so bad? There's more glory in smacking proactively into an iceberg than being smacked into by a taxicab. I try to remember what happens when you drown. Is it as merciful a situation as dying in a fire, where you pass out from smoke inhalation before you're burned alive?

The car stops. We are propelled forward again, and then flopped against our seatbacks, and then . . . nothing.

No glass shattering. No explosion. I feel my face, checking off features with my fingertips. As I drop my hand and stare forward, I realize that our car is not the problem. The problem is the pickup truck ahead of us, which has flung itself from a side road and is ahead of us. Its driver is clearly drunk and swerving wildly. If anyone needs to be having half-second death fantasies, it's this guy.

A baby brown bear comes ambling out of the woods. As Jeff's cursing echoes in my head, my newly acquired vocabulary kicks in, momentarily translating "shit" to "scat." But after the word zips around, it lands on my primary definition of "scat." I think: *Run, little bear, run.*

But there's no time. The truck plows straight into the cub. The driver speeds off in the same direction he approached (i.e., a sampling of all of them). The noise of the bear being hit is actually not so bad. But the visual isn't doing my denial any favors. The bear rolls next to our car and goes limp, a mound of fetal fur moving up and down, but barely. We gasp in unison, the sound of our warning bells banging against our necks. As we crane to see if the bear is still breathing, April and Jeff spring out of the car. Even for them, this scene is unusual. They flank the bear on either side, preparing to hail oncoming traffic to prevent it from getting hit twice. But no traffic comes. Jeff calls the park service, and we wait. There's no telling how long it will take them to get out here. The animal attempts to distance itself from a widening puddle of blood, leaning on one arm for a moment before collapsing in exhaustion. He can't seem to grasp why the bones and cartilage and muscle that were working so well a moment ago will no longer hold. The blood is growing darker, so that it looks like a flat extension of his fur. It is easily the most upsetting thing I have ever seen.

"I hit a moose in Montana once," one of the bridesmaids says, trying to help.

Everyone turns to look at her. She starts to speak again but doesn't. There's nothing to say. A moose is worse for one's car, but it's ultimately much less cute.

Oh, no.

I seek out the cuddly paw fanatic, and sure enough, her bottom lip is trembling. She can't hold back. She starts crying.

"It'll be okay," says the moose killer.

No, it won't.

The girl becomes hysterical. But in the wrong direction. She worries that the bear will cryogenically heal and become rabid. Having seen her apply a similar level of concern over an egg omelet with cheese on top, which was supposed to be an egg-white omelet with cheese on the side, I assume her panic will subside at any moment. Instead, her words become increasingly nonsensical, a mixed bag of ranting and dramatic gasps that hack away at my sympathy for the bear. "It's not that big a deal," I want to yell. Except that it is that big a deal. My resentment is rising. I am trying to absorb the situation and would like to do my absorption in peace. In general, I prefer to record all traumas and save them for later, playing them over and over so they can haunt me for a disproportionate number of weeks to come. It's very healthy.

I turn away from her and try to concentrate on the bear, who has now put his baby snout flat to the pavement, his eyes and nose forming a trinity of black spots that look up, searching for a spot on which to fixate. This is more nature than we bargained for, to be sure. Exactly how much more? I find myself longing for yesterday, when I was intimidated by trail mix.

Hysterical Girl continues to be so. I roll down the window, and April leans over me and holds her hand, trying to calm her down, but it's no use. She frenzies herself into a dull mumble, leans over my lap, and implores April and Jeff to get back in the car. She screams as though gathering the troops to retreat on the beaches of Normandy. I rub my ear. I am on the verge of slapping her, convinced it's the humane thing to do, when she pauses and, with the support of a giant heaving breath, belts out: *"What about the mama?!"*

They say if you give a monkey enough time, he'll type Shakespeare. Presumably, you'd have to give him a typewriter as well. But that's neither here nor there. Either way, the same is true for the neurotic. I whip around and blink at her, my bear bell following me.

"She makes a solid point," I say to April.

When a squirrel makes a poorly timed highway excursion, I am not particularly concerned about its mother emerging from a tree to gouge my eyes out. A bear is another matter. This road cuts straight through a thick forest. Mama can't be far off. And if the punishment for picking a wildflower is scalping, there's no way crippling a cub has a lenient ending. April gets back into the car, her face red and scrunched. She wipes her eyes on her sleeve. Jeff is still on the phone with the park service, looking out for nonexistent traffic.

"Did anyone get the license plate?" he shouts.

"958XPO," I recite. Everyone turns and glares at me, possibly even the bear.

"What?" I look around. "I grew up in the burbs. We were all afraid of getting kidnapped. I used to memorize the license plates of shady vans."

I may not know how to gut a salmon or BeDazzle a gun case, but I am not without my skills.

Just then a car pulls up behind ours, and a man in a Navy Seals T-shirt and green fishing hat emerges. He adjusts the hat as he walks forward. He adopts a "What seems to be the problem here?" swagger that feels out of place. The problem is apparent, the picture painted: baby bear, injured, blood on pavement. The man and Jeff stand over the bear. The introduction of a stranger somehow reactivates the hysterics of the passenger to my right.

"Oh my God," she snorts. "What's he doing here?"

I don't know, driving home? Making waffles? It's his state, not ours. What are *we* doing here? I can feel the tingling in my hand as if I've already slapped her, so right does it feel. Before I left for Alaska, my sister told me to (a) fly safe and (b) watch out because "I hear everyone has a gun." I glare at our sniffler. Now, I think, would be such a good time for that to be true. Although after her last revelation I wonder if she sees something I don't. Perhaps danger has a color. Perhaps this man's aura is flashing neon red and is visible only to unnerved women. Meanwhile, the conversation on the road is growing heated. I make a move to get up, only to realize I've had my seat belt fastened this whole time. By the time I unbuckle it, the man has taken a wide step toward the bear.

"Hey," I say, surprised at the sound of my own voice.

The bear tries to get up once again, this time with less

success and the bonus indignity of defecation. We are help-
less as goldfish behind the SUV's glass. The man lifts the
back of his T-shirt to reveal a small holster. He removes a
handgun and shoots the bear point-blank in the head four
times.

The blood goes black.

Our bells are silenced.

The sound of gunshots reverberates off the tree trunks
and rocks around us. I wonder about avalanche triggers.
There's a collective whimper in the car. I have always wondered what I would do if I was in one of those movies where
someone gets stabbed or eaten alive while I'm in the closet or
under the bed. The last thing one wants is to be unprepared
when one walks into the bathroom to find their spouse has
been making toast on the ledge of the bathtub *again*. Now I
know. I would do nothing. I would just stare. Make a note of
it and replay it later.

Which I will, and recklessly. I know each time I tell this
story, I damage my memory of it. Each time it moves a little
further away from what happened. The visuals are fading,
merging what dead animal fur looks like and what I *think*
dead animal fur looks like. I remember the polar bears in the
zoo and think perhaps it's just a bear-specific issue. All stories involving bears and blood are subject to literal and mental disfiguration. And yet I can't resist the retelling. Look
how *real* Alaska got. Look at the beauty and the beasts. More
than one person will react by saying, "Nice how everyone in

Alaska has a gun in their car." Prior to my arctic excursion I would have dismissed this as a gross generalization. Now I nod. *Yes. Nice.*

I took one hundred thirty-two photographs in Alaska, one hundred of which are of icebergs. Sometimes you can see otters or fishing poles in the background. Sometimes you can see the Ghost Forests, betraying their vampire-like nature by showing up in pictures. Mostly it's a lot of ice. I blind people with iceberg photos. Here's an iceberg from far away. Here it is again, up close. Here's a chunk of it floating in the water. Here it is from the boat, from the shore, from the side, give me cold, give me big, you're chiseled like an ice sculpture, you're a cube and the ocean is your glass. Brrr, baby, brrrr. The pictures are frustrating.

What I want to say is: Here is a country that is ours but not ours. A crazed landscape of death and marriage with designated bells to acknowledge both. Here is the longest breath of fresh air you will ever take, the bluest stream you will ever dip your hand in, the humane thing to do. Here is my friend, who I miss so much. I may have found new people with new novelties, perhaps even better suited to my own. But none to go kayaking on the Hudson with me. None to look up more than they look down. None to remind me that this is, and has always been, the real world as long as people are here to witness it. Why does none of it show up on film? Maybe I just need a better camera.

If You Sprinkle

So shines a good deed in a weary world.

—SHAKESPEARE, VIA *Charlie and the Chocolate Factory*

I had little red circles stuck to my chin, cheeks, and forehead when Zooey Ellis warned us that Rachel Hermann was going to be joining our slumber party. We sat in a circle as Zooey instructed us to be extra-sensitive because Rachel was new to school. And because she had two mommies. No one, under any circumstances, was to bring this up. Nor were we to acknowledge this abomination of a situation by encouraging Rachel to bring it up. Giving credence to this unnatural and—let's face it—unfashionable union would risk making Rachel "feel the shame a child of her age should never have to feel." Zooey's parents were Republicans.

I nodded in unison with the rest of the girls, memorizing Mrs. Ellis's words as they funneled forth from a miniature version of her pouty mouth. One of the red stickers came loose from my chin and fell on the carpet. I plucked it up, pinching it in my nail bed, but when I went to put it back on,

I saw that its minuscule circumference was already covered with carpet fibers. So I sat on it instead. The sticker, meant to double as a "zit," was part of a board game called Girl Talk, an early-'90s version of truth-or-dare, designed to sanction prepubescent cruelty via laminated cardboard. Accompanying the board itself were zits peeled from an adhesive sheet and doled out to those who refused to participate in dares. Imagine the karmic opposite of candy dots. Girl Talk was the main reason I wound up enrolling in a college without a Greek system.

The game began by spinning a plastic arrow so cheap and lopsided that you didn't "spin" it so much as flick it very fast. The arrow touched down in one of four pie-shaped categories of clairvoyance:

MARRIAGE

CHILDREN

CAREER

SPECIAL MOMENTS

The whole concept of forecasting and fortune telling was very en vogue at the time, often taking the form of origami finger puppets that told you when you'd lose your virginity and where you'd live when you grew up. Soda-can tabs predicted the first letter of your future husband's name, candles melted to reveal secret scrolls, moods were exposed depending on the temperature of your ring finger. The future was everywhere, and it was all very illuminating. Girl Talk simply did the grunt work for you, its forecasting preprinted on triangular cards that fit into the board like the courses in TV dinner entrées.

To its credit, Girl Talk was downright empowering compared to Mall Madness, a game of fiscal responsibility that encouraged girls to buy everything in sight until they found a boy to do it for them. Girl Talk was also strangely complicated, a layered enterprise with rules complex enough to make the ancient Chinese game of Go look like Candy Land. Before you put your fate in the hands of a plastic wheel, you had a choice. You could either tell the truth or pick from a series of dares. These ranged from the coy ("Call a boy and ask him who he likes") to the suspect ("Act like Pee-wee Herman for one minute") to the dehumanizing ("Lap up a bowl of water like a dog").

Imagine, if you will, the legal repercussions of a game manufactured today in which underage girls are encouraged to call strangers' homes in the middle of the night. Or to leave the house sporting a "silly outfit." It's all fun and games until someone winds up in the back of a cop car, clutching a Cabbage Patch Kid. In hindsight, I am proud that I declined to imitate a convicted child molester or assume a doggie position in order to win a board game. As if all this wasn't enough, you needed "household" items to play, including shoelaces, a short-wave radio, and a blindfold. Were we preparing for our future fiancés or the apocalypse? Or both?

The Special Moments cards were far and away my favorite. Even as kids, we recognized the dated presumption that all our special moments would have to be found *outside* the colored wedges of Marriage or Career. Nope, no joy there. Cue the visual of grown Girl Talk players, seeking out their "special moments" by going on shopping sprees beyond their means, binge-eating their children's Easter candy, and sitting on dressing room benches, trying on La Perla underwear and weeping. . . .

It's easy to point at the past and say, "Can you believe we ever thought this was okay?" It makes one wonder what contemporary nuggets of idiocy we're producing. What we call "normal" now will eventually be viewed as cultural carbon monoxide—the silent killer of logic and good sense, imperceptible until we all wake up in ten years surrounded by photos of women wearing sunglasses sized for bullmastiffs on their way to stick vials of stroke medication into their eyebrows. Looking back, I can't decide which makes me cringe more—that I avoided speaking to Rachel Hermann about her home life or that I participated in a game that predicted the number of babies I would one day expel from my body as dictated by the first digit of my area code. That would be nine. Who wrote this shit? Mormons?

If I had been permitted to ask Rachel questions, I'm not sure what they would have been. But what I can say is what they wouldn't have been. They wouldn't have been about the devil's musical stylings that were the Indigo Girls. Or hemp. Or why one of her mothers wore gym shorts in the middle of winter. I wished I could spin an arrow and it could land on a new category called Reality. I wondered: What was Rachel's life like? What did she make of us? Did she have to put stickers on her face and drink from a dog bowl where she came from? If you have two mommies, can you still play one parent off the other? Were you saddled with two bad cops or blessed with two pushovers?

"Hey"—one of Zooey's minions poked me in the biceps—"I think you're missing a zit."

She bounced her index finger in close proximity to my face, counting my battle scars. Then she consulted the rule-book, searching for a punishment for the intentional smuggling of fake pimples.

For all its many flaws—and there were many—at Girl Talk's core was the single lesson that prepared me for truth-or-dare. Which prepared me for "I never." A thread of advice that strung through all the drinking games of New England and, subsequently, life as I know it. I learned that if you want to get out of something, it is always better to tell the truth. Not because it is the moral option, but because nine times out of ten, it's less work. The path of least resistance. Turn the pockets of your past inside out, beat your peers to the punch, expose yourself, and bore the people around you into leaving you be. Two-mommied Rachel knew this, too.

When she arrived after dark, it somehow made sense

that she would be dropped off later than everyone else, that her parents parented differently than ours did. Not so much because there were multiple sets of breasts involved, but because Rachel had just moved to the East Coast from California. What the time difference didn't account for, the Berkeley mentality did. "Seven p.m." was more of a suggestion than a fact.

Rachel was tall for our age, lanky, with wide-set eyes that would be identified by any modeling scout as "Jackie O–like" but which were identified by our peers as Kermit-like. She had already begun to hunch. If I have ever come to the defense of a celebrity who claims to have been called Olive Oyl or Skeletor as a child, Rachel is the reason. But for all her physical discomfort, she had a sense of calm about her. Her voice, which never surpassed a certain octave, made me conscious of keeping my own exaggerated squeaks to a minimum. She seemed a bit older and a lot wiser than we were, the way people who have lived elsewhere seem when you're twelve years old. If I could make a graph of our miniature society, charting how much Rachel spoke, how many stories and crushes of her own she shared, how many times she complimented other girls, Rachel would fall exactly in the center. Over the next few years, she landed in this spot with apparent effortlessness. Whereas my endeavors to fit in were always soaked with effort. Alas, taking stock after each chauffeured trip to the movies and each sleepover, I calculated too many failed jokes, too little volume control, or too much forced mysterious silence on my part. Or, worst of all, zero attention from Zooey.

Aside from the twenty-five-year-old fresh-man, the most unrealistic aspect of teen movies is how conscious the upper echelons are of their own status. Whereas in real life, such hyper-awareness of group dynamic would only damage one's social standing. Cafeteria tables may be as delineated as nation-states, but the borders remain invisible at all times. Getting caught muttering Shakespearean monologues about one's plans for coup-staging would make you seem schizophrenic. When it comes to pointing out middle-school injustice, it's not just impolite to point—it's unproductive. At the time I thought we were all conscious of this system, undetectable to the naked eye as it was. As it turns out, the bird's-eye view of grade school is not to be found at the top of the tree. The altitude of popularity actually makes you a little stupid.

I know this because in adult life, I am friendly with a girl who would have been portrayed as a Queen Bee in any teen drama but at the time clearly thought of herself as, say, an affable ladybug. A Marie Antoinette figure who unconsciously abused and misunderstood her position. Oblivious to the system, she assumed that the populace of other cliques was composed of people who shared different interests, who she just didn't know as well. Recently she said to me, "Can you believe it? Craig Marcos got divorced."

I scrolled through the contact list in my head until I produced an image the approximate size and shape of someone named Craig Marcos.

I said, "Craig Marcos got married?"

The blithe assumption that I kept tabs on her friends, that I'd be invested in their contemporary lives, would be insulting if it wasn't so flattering. She viewed her world not in cliques but as this borderless mass of fun where the only reason she might not see you at a secret party was because you were across town at an even better and more secret party. It was downright touching. How can you not want to hug Marie Antoinette just a little bit when she suggests replacing bread with cake? It's made of sugar and flour. It's not like it's a *bad* idea.

Zooey was a different animal. One got the feeling she was abnormally aware of her power within this falsely inclusive echelon. But she would never wield it against me. Not because I had done anything especially cool to warrant my turn skipped in that great Girl Talk game of life. I simply had too much on her.

The incident had taken place in fifth grade, a time when I was regularly raising my hand and asking for the bathroom hall pass during math class. The "pass" was a normal-sized key with a wooden block the size of a brick attached to it. This was meant to broadcast the administration's lack of faith in our ability to hold on to small objects. Still, I would rather clutch in my hand that corroded block, which every child who didn't wash his or her hands had just clutched, than spend half an hour writing numbers on a blackboard. Afflicted with the plight of the right-brained, I had no gift for percentages or protractors. I raised my hand for the hall pass with increasing frequency.

I'd wander around the school grounds, kicking acorns on the concrete beneath the basketball net and stopping to appreciate the big mural outside the auditorium. Little did I know I was about two pee-break excursions away from my math teacher calling my mother and my mother calling a doctor, who would quiz me on my frequent urination habits. I felt at once empowered by and guilty about the perception my teachers and parents had of me, that of a child whose devious acts were not the stuff of white lies but the stuff of white coats. Surely there must be some terrible force beyond my control causing me to skip class. Testing negative for everything, the doctor left me with the suggestion that I "wipe more thoroughly," a piece of advice that has stayed with me to this day, despite the fact that I was being misdiagnosed at the time it was given.

What I had was an acute case of procrastination. When Mattel released its infamous "Math is hard!" Barbie doll, the woman cut to the core of me. To my mind, the only flaw in her design was that she didn't say "Math is hard!" and then spontaneously raise her hand via some battery-powered mechanism in her plastic rotator cuff. (I think she also said something to the effect of "Let's go shopping!" But the math crack was so insanely sexist, Barbie's minor faux pas got lost between the cracks of the Dream House floorboards.)

I was taking one of my regular constitutionals around the halls, clutching the pass and sidestepping the discolored spots of tile, which were known to have a high concentration of cooties. I snooped in the supply closet, which held only makeshift aisles of paper reams and boxes of No. 2 pencils but in which I fantasized were hidden secret documents implicating the school in a national scandal. Or, at the very least, the blueprints of the building, which would at long last prove it was an exact replica of a medieval dungeon.

By this time I actually had to pee. I walked into the girls' room and did a quick visual sweep under the stalls. I was going through a phase where I felt uncomfortable when people could hear me going to the bathroom. I'm still going through it, really. Problems arise when the biological and the social get too close. Why do people persist in carrying on a conversation from the adjoining stall, forcing me to flush on them mid-sentence? It's amazing that we listen to one another release piss and excrement into porcelain tubs and then pretend like nothing happened. We hear the difference between a healthy digestive system and one that has been plied with beer and cheese fries the previous night. It's not that I desperately longed to have open conversations about bowels and pus and mucus. I had a roommate like that once, who used to stare quizzically at the food globules on her used dental floss and encouraged me to do the same. I no longer live with this person.

My eyes stopped sweeping when I saw two tie-dyed Keds with blue ink tattooed around each sole. The fringes of a pair of stonewashed jeans covered the laces. Zooey. I opened the stall adjacent to hers, made myself a toilet-paper wreath, and sat. I enjoyed the idea of catching Zooey being human, even if it meant I had to listen to someone in the next stall. I also enjoyed the anonymity. I imagined her feeling as embarrassed as I would have been.

"*Owwwwum,*" she whimpered. "*Ow o wow. Hooooof.*"

Silence again. Followed by a throat clear.

"*O wow ow,* shit, *ow,*" she whimpered, louder this time. Something was very wrong.

"Zooey?"

My voice was tentative as a ream of toilet paper rolled on the ground from one stall to the next. She slid her feet closer together until the rubber bumpers of her Keds touched.

"Everything okay in there?"

At the unripe age of ten and three quarters, Zooey's body had gone ahead and won itself the distinction of first period in our class. Despite her mother's encouragement to stick with the "less interfering" feminine hygiene products, Zooey was ready to take on the tampon. I was listening to the sound track of her first attempt. A process that sounded so atrocious that when my time came years later, I thought of nothing but. I practiced the art of relaxing my own muscles by lying on my bed and pretending someone had just knocked me unconscious with a frying pan, conveniently anesthetizing every nerve in my body except the ones in my right arm.

Zooey was not used to being embarrassed, and thus had no storage container for her shame. She had no practice in suppressing awkward moments the way the rest of us had. Instead, it kind of free-form spread all over her like a rash.

"Please, *please,* don't tell anyone," she implored, her voice extra-breathy and high.

Who would I tell? I couldn't imagine. Where would "Zooey's bleeding like a stuck pig" fit into a conversation about the merits of wall clocks in the shape of Swatch watches?

"I won't, I swear."

We were at that age when it's difficult to imagine others not thinking as you do. I assumed Zooey was paranoid about en masse urination because I was paranoid about en masse urination. Likewise, she asked me to keep her secret because if it had been *me* trying to negotiate with a cotton missile, she would have told everyone by lunchtime.

I coached her via the Lamaze breathing techniques I had seen in talking-baby movies. Not in possession of a stick to bite, Zooey reached her non-nether-region-exploring hand under the stall for me to grab. I hesitated on hygienic grounds, unsure if that expression about one hand not knowing what the other is doing could be applied so literally.

"I'm just going to get it over with." She wiggled her fingers again.

Not only was this a bonding moment between Zooey and me but a much-needed bonding moment between Zooey and the rest of womankind. I reached down and squeezed the hand of Zooey Ellis as she inserted her first tampon.

We walked out of the girls' room in silence, passing the supply room and making a right at the classroom where M.A.S.P. met. M.A.S.P. was an acronym for "More Able Student Program." The administration has since changed it to S.O.A.R., which presumably expands into a more polite label than "Other People's Children Are Idiots." Before we parted ways, we stopped and glanced through the square window in the door. Neither Zooey nor I were in M.A.S.P. Through the window we saw kids gathered in organic clumps, chatting. We moved in closer. One day soon this group would include Rachel Hermann. Rachel, who would laugh and gesticulate in a way she never did when she was with us. In a smattering of seldom-seen instances of bonding, Zooey and I would spy on Rachel. We would watch as Rachel regaled the room with her stories, commanding the attention of anyone in her orbit. Perhaps the fellow geniuses brought out the girl in Rachel Hermann, whereas fellow girls brought out the quiet genius. I remember watching Zooey watch Rachel. As she glared, I realized that her profile was the perfect facsimile of one of the smiling and wicked teenage photos that graced the old Girl Talk box. So many rules crammed into such a pixie-sized head.

Did I want to be Zooey Ellis? I think mostly I just didn't want to be in her way.

One night I found myself sitting on the floor of my room on the phone with her. I sensed the conversation was winding down for her, and my own bedtime loomed large. I scrunched my toes around the cord. I didn't want her to hang up and have our final topic of conversation be about my family's trip to Williamsburg, Virginia. A trip in which my sister locked me in a stockade and my cousin almost broke a colonial lantern.

"Did he break it?" Her impatience was thicker than sound.

"He almost broke it. He tripped and fell onto the velvet rope. It almost fell on the ground. It was really funny."

"So then he didn't get in trouble."

"It wobbled."

In a last-ditch effort, I became instinctively Machiavellian, preying on the weakest social link I could think of. I knew that Zooey had put an extraordinary amount of effort into being politically correct around Rachel. But I also knew that she didn't particularly like Rachel. She didn't particularly *like* anyone. All she needed was a striking point, some flaw in Rachel located at a safe distance from the lack of penis in her household. I confided—speculated, really— that Rachel did not actually appear to be from California.

"She's really pale. And she doesn't know how to surf. Which would be like not knowing how to ice-skate."

"I don't know how to ice-skate." Zooey remained unconvinced.

"But you don't walk out your front door onto an ice-skating rink. Everyone in California has a view of the ocean."

The well of bogus logic from which one can draw as a preteen is bottomless. With that jet-black hair and those non-cornflower eyes, Rachel didn't hail from the Christie Brinkley school of sunshine and tooth enamel. Zooey perked up. I had successfully superimposed my own ignorance of the West Coast onto Rachel until my incomplete image of her background made her incomplete as a person.

In a matter of days the rumor spread, hopping like a cootie from one person to the next until one afternoon Zooey confronted her. As Rachel waited for one of her many moms to pick her up in the parking lot, Zooey tapped her on the shoulder and began baiting her, quizzing her about the California state flower. When Rachel shrugged, Zooey moved on to the bird, the gemstone, the fish, the vegetable. And the crowds, they gathered. Rachel was desperate to prove her origins, which seems like it would be simple enough. But this was before driver's licenses, before library cards, before wallet-sized photos, before wallets period. We knew not the names of the highways on which we were driven nor the prices once we arrived at the local food chain that was, unbeknownst to us, local. Even quarters were just quarters, not yet embossed with state-specific horses and peaches. It was terrible, watching Rachel dig for relics in her backpack, pulling out a half-empty pack of Nerds (the flavor of which she claimed was not distributed on the East Coast) and a neon ruler she had brought with her, and finally holding up her wrist to show us the rainbow hemp bracelets that would stay there until they disintegrated.

There is a keen need for evidence when you are young. My need was fed by watching my older sister, who had spades of evidence of being cool. The frayed sweatshirts from her hockey-team-captain boyfriend. The concert ticket stubs. The photos of her and her friends slumped against a brick wall outside the movies with their arms draped around one another. It was enough to make you wonder who did their blocking. But you didn't need an older sister for social show-and-tell. You just needed to live in the world.

Zooey grabbed the ruler from Rachel's hand.

"Then how do you explain *this*?" she hissed, gesturing at the damning lettering on the back: MADE IN CHINA.

Before she could respond, Rachel's mother arrived. I could see her already starting to cry as they pulled out of the rounded driveway. I could also see the resemblance—this mommy was her biological mommy. A free hand reached around to squeeze her daughter's shoulder.

It occurs to me now that instead of flying into the passenger seat, all Rachel had to do was march over to the California plates on the car and point. Even as an adult, I am still looking for ways for her to win that fight. How can we not still be rooting for the younger versions of ourselves as if they actually exist, playing catch-up in time? Who wouldn't like to implant their current brains into a scenario from the past? SATs be damned, how about the insertion of a few eloquent turns of phrase when, for no discernible reason, Michael Gruzman called me "baloney boobs" on the bus home for a whole year? At the time I could only fold my arms over my mild-mammaried chest and stare out the window, wishing I had the superhuman strength required to slide open one of those school-bus windows and push Michael Gruzman out of it. Surely now I could at least eke out a "Shut it, assclown." Or match the boys in physical development jokes, quoting Truman Capote when he was asked to sign a man's penis: "I couldn't sign it, but perhaps I could initial it?"

Oh, yes, I could have sixth grade on a string. And if I did, I would stop the tape, rewind, and flick the big plastic arrow of time to point Rachel in the direction of her mother's license plates.

AS TIME PASSED AND MORE OF OUR PEERS JOINED Zooey in the Active Uterus Club, I became less exempt from her wrath. Zooey's prior embarrassment had been alleviated by the acquisition of breasts and the subsequent attention and confidence they provided. She was a well-oiled machine of lady. My own body, meanwhile, was about as functional as the combination lock on my locker, which refused to do as it was told. By eighth grade, it seemed that the crimson wave had swept through every fallopian tube but mine.

It was only a matter of time before Zooey caught on to the mootness of our friendship. In the matter of personal injury, she could be exceedingly vicious and random, like a tornado touching down at untraceable intervals. One day, after the janitor had to pry open my actual locker, I found Zooey had cut different-sized and -colored letters out of her *Seventeen* and *YM* magazines, gotten out her rubber cement, and crafted what looked like a ransom note:

YoU R a Looser.

I had several elements on my side, spell-check among them. I also questioned the choice of "ransom" as a note-leaving genre. I stood agape in the hallway, my shoulders as slouched as my socks, thinking: And? Was there no price to pay? I flipped the note over, anticipating a "thus your entire pencil collection must be left in the earth-science cubbies by noon oR ElSe." But the other side was just a mess of glue outlines. Then the note's ingenuity dawned on me. It managed to combine both threat and punishment in one. Like a parking ticket. Zooey abruptly stopped being my friend. And there was no challenging a verdict like that. Her rules were tighter than her vagina.

It was not a bad thing when Zooey's family moved to Arizona. She hadn't spoken to me for years. Which wasn't so different from when she was speaking to me. Her daily presence was like a wolf's glowing eyes in the woods. It might not be chewing your face off right this very minute, but you felt a hell of a lot better when it was gone. Unsurprisingly, the top triangle on the food pyramid was self-regenerating. But no girl who assumed the apex had the power and prestige of a Zooey Ellis. As it is with all political movements, after the social unrest has settled, after the statue is removed from the square, the rose-colored nostalgia begins. Who would pass notes about us now? Who would rule recess with an iron Trapper Keeper? Would white T-shirts under strappy floral dresses have been permitted under Zooey's regime?

The world may never know. But high school happened without her, and it wasn't that bad. It wasn't that good, either. But at least I could go to the bathroom safe in the knowledge that all my major biological developments had come to pass. There was no longer a need to confess the details of each other's private space. So much real was happening outside the stall door, it became difficult to hold on to frivolous paranoias. Fear of physical exposure (noogies, pantsings, spitballs, defecation) gave way to fear of social exposure (crushes, rejections, awkward friendship transgressions). I scanned for feet with decreased frequency. Until I didn't at all. I just went to the bathroom like a normal person.

EIGHTY-FOUR CYCLES LATER I FOUND MYSELF standing in the ladies' room of a Burger King on East 116th Street, holding a notepad in one hand and a can of pepper spray disguised as a tube of lipstick in the other.

I was spending the semester at Columbia University, and I approached my first stint as a New York City resident with the wide-eyed verve of a midwesterner. Except that, unlike a midwesterner, I did it with the intention of obscuring the wide-eyed-ness as quickly as possible. I did not go up to the Statue of Liberty's crown to marvel at the view so much as to get it over with. Having grown up within spitting distance of the city (you can see the Empire State Building from White Plains—so not too long an arc of metaphorical saliva), I was playing catch-up with New York. Now that I was one of its residents, I sought out the best bagels and pizza and shoe-repair places. I took the M4 up to the Cloisters to see the tapestries, so far up I was the only one on the bus except for Sigourney Weaver and her kids, who sat quietly in the back, wearing black sunglasses and sharing a soft pretzel. I bought the most expensive and ugliest dress I had ever seen at the old Patricia Field's on Eighth Street. I wore it to a Saint A's formal, where I drank too many vodka tonics and stole a bottle of liquid soap for no good reason. I knew the one palm reader in Chinatown who could actually tell me my future. Gone were the days of finger origami and Coke cans. My lifeline is long and my money and love lines are broken, and thus I will likely become a drunken hobo and die alone. Which sounds about right.

I took women's studies classes at Barnard, which were at once strangely empowering and completely useless. Every student's spin on feminist theory was left unchecked, thrown into some pot of higher learning, the bland mixture then poured back into our professor's dissertation. Every paragraph was read twice before you realized you had already read it. Even when a piece of understanding could be shaken out, it seemed to float away in a sea of "ethical gender systems." It was like panning for gold on the moon. *Shake, shake, oh! There's one. And there it goes. . . .* But I loved it because I was in New York. I had urban bulimia—I wanted to gobble up the city so I could throw it back up as quickly as possible and start over.

To cap off my immersion, I took an urban anthropology class. For our final exam, we had to do "fieldwork." Successful projects of years past had included interviewing MTA officials and especially hostile homeless people. I decided to employ the lessons of my women's studies class and my general wonderment of the city to explore the cross-socioeconomic behavioral patterns of women's lavatories.

There's a very limited amount of things one can do in the bathroom while still operating within the bounds of normalcy. I will go ahead and tell you that skulking for hours on end with a notebook under your arm, periodically setting off the automated hand dryer, is not one of those things. More than once I stood by as women shook water from their hands, waiting for me to hand them a paper towel. Occasionally, I obliged.

This behavior mostly occurred in the more posh bathrooms. The bathroom at Henri Bendel, for example, didn't have stalls but individual rooms with walls that went straight to the floor. The doors to these rooms were expertly rounded, the kind you imagine Alice passing through on her way to Wonderland. The "ladies' lounge" even had an upholstered bench for me to sit on while taking notes. It's funny what rich people will tell you. During the middle of the day on Fifth Avenue, when the trophy wives come out to play, they feel compelled to connect. At one point a blonde in her late thirties for which the word "statuesque" was invented emerged from one of Bendel's gilded rabbit holes. She was rearranging her bangs in the mirror when she abruptly turned to me.

"Can I show you something?" She leaned in quizzically. She tilted her head and blinked rapidly, as the python dyed purple for her bag might have done in its better days. At first I did not realize she was addressing me. It was as if I was painting a still life, so obsessed with capturing the sheen on an apple that I didn't notice it had walked out of the bowl and started speaking.

"Sure." I slid my pen into the spiral binding of my notebook and walked over to the paper towel dispenser.

"No, over here." She gestured, pulling me in.

"Lend me this?" She rested her hand on my shoulder without waiting for a reply. With her other hand she removed her heel to reveal a set of mangled toes. Toes so welt-covered and deformed, they looked as if they'd been grafted from a cadaver onto her otherwise perfect body. The pinkie toe, most innocent of appendages, was in especially bad shape.

"Gross," I whispered reflexively, repulsed but transfixed by the colors of it all.

"The price of beauty, right?" She looked me up and down, ready to commiserate, but was clearly disappointed by what she found. Which was a college student in ripped jeans and clogs. I hadn't plucked my eyebrows for a week, and a graveyard of hair elastics formed around my wrist, many with hairs tangled in them. She let go of my shoulder and leaned on the marble sink instead.

"The pinkie's the worst. What do you think that thing is?"

"A wart?"

"No, it's not a *wart*."

She was incredulous. If I was going to be this unkempt and slovenly, the least I could do was be an expert in foot deformations.

"Maybe it's a blister. Have you tried popping it?"

"You know, that's probably what it is." She hopped on one foot while trying to get a closer look at the other.

"You don't think I have to go to the doctor to pop a blister, do I? I can't have strangers touching my feet."

"I say pop it. It's just a layer of skin, it won't scar. I've done it before."

"Really?" She hopped.

"It's a strangely rewarding thing to do."

I then watched as my words morphed in slow motion from suggestion to invitation. She unzipped a pocket inside her bag, produced a safety pin, and proudly handed it to me.

"Care to do the honors?"

"No, thank you." I handed her a paper towel.

I got out onto the sidewalk and leaned against the jeweled windows of Harry Winston, furiously scribbling down the scene I had just witnessed. My paper was due in just a few days. The sky was as dark as a rich lady's big toe. I had been writing in my notebook since noon and was beginning to test the resolve of my dromedary-like bladder. A bad habit I had retained from my hall-pass days. So, after a day of hanging out in bathrooms and paradoxically never going to the bathroom, I ducked into one at random.

It was in the back of a Chinese restaurant. I put on my best "I ate here earlier and left my scarf in the back booth" face. Against a pastel wall of the restroom were cheaply framed photographs of vegetable lo mein, whole fish fillets, and an especially unappetizing composition involving egg drop soup and a whole octopus. I've never met a restaurant photograph of food I liked, and these were no exception. They were hung directly above the toilets, as if meant to alert future civilizations to our digestive process. I popped into the stall farthest from the door and slid the lock with my sleeve yanked over my left hand. I faced a line of graffiti poetry I hadn't seen since summer camp: *If you sprinkle when you tinkle, please be neat and wipe the seat*. As a kid, this was etched in ballpoint on wood, just for the sake of the rhyme. As an adult, it struck me as a rather helpful tip. Thank you, Midtown restaurant toilet, for acknowledging that you are too disgusting for direct contact with human flesh and must be hovered over.

As I finished up, I noticed two new sets of feet, one much smaller than the other, in the adjoining stall. The voice belonging to the larger set was narrating.

"So you've wiped and pulled your pants up. Now what?"

"I flush!"

"You flush!"

I ducked my head down. The larger feet were wearing expensive-looking gold sandals with beads that ran down the center of the foot like a spine. The smaller set bounced up and down, periodically causing red lights to explode from the rubber heels.

So many years and miles away from the second-floor girls' room where Zooey Ellis used her first tampon, her voice was unmistakable.

My mouth dropped open. Was she not supposed to be in Arizona, fending off scorpions and practicing her golf swing? It's difficult to conceive of the geography of the whole wide world when you're in middle school. When your classmates move away, it seems impossible that they could ever come back. As if the world's events since have happened to you but not to them. It's the reason you can look at your middle-school yearbook and still see your peers. But someone else's middle-school yearbook looks like a bunch of thirteen-year-olds. Did I expect to find a prison anklet as I looked askance at the feet? It's not like the woman was under house arrest. She was allowed to leave the state. And to breed, it would seem.

Zooey's voice had such a visceral effect on me, I sat directly on the toilet seat and lifted my legs. I kept them like that, in midair. When I used to have flying dreams as a kid, I would never go higher than this. In the dreams, I would run to gain momentum and then tuck my legs up. As long as I squeezed my abdominal muscles, I would be able to hover a few feet above the ground. I remember telling Zooey this once while we were on the cafeteria lunch line. She said my lack of soaring meant I had a limited subconscious and easily thwarted goals.

I heard Zooey and mini-Zooey exit their stall. I had a choice to make. Did I want to run into her again? If I did, I had better act fast. What if I waited too long and missed her or, worse, what if I waited so long to exit the stall that it looked like I was having some sort of gastrointestinal emergency? All my life's accomplishments fade away, and on the subject of how I'm doing, Zooey's only reference is that I have diarrhea in Chinese restaurants.

"Zooey Ellis," I said, almost accusatory.

As it is with anyone who has made an impact on your life, her first and last name are inseparable. The metal door bounced against the frame behind me.

Zooey had not changed much. She had the same freckled face, inky hair, and blue eyes. There were lines around her neck but none around her eyes, which I took to mean she had been doing little smiling and much awkward looking down at the ground. But she was beautiful. If this were a movie, she wouldn't have been. Her feet would have been a red herring. From the ankles up, she would have packed on the pounds and developed some adult acne. Maybe there would be an oversized scorpion tattoo jiggling on her upper arm. She would have giddily told me about her repetitive days cataloging defective remote controls for the cable company and how she plays our video yearbook on the flat-screen TV at the bowling alley, where she always has her birthday parties.

Alas, this was not a movie. Zooey Ellis was well under two hundred pounds, smelled fine, and was enrolled in college. But she did have a kid with her. Her daughter was an exact replica, except blond and significantly shorter. She held on to her mother's leg with one hand and hid behind her calf. My thoughts were especially graphic when I looked at this little girl, as my strongest memory of Zooey Ellis pertained to the logistics of her being a woman. The whole phrase "guess Zooey learned to stick more than a tampon up there" passed through my brain like a news crawl.

"Oh my God, Sloane, hi!" And she hugged me, the miniature human still attached to her calf. "Do you live here?"

Do I live here? Do *I* live here? Damn skippy I live here, you Marie Antoinette, you.

"I'm uptown."

"Ah, I'm just visiting Emma here."

The child called Emma had since dislodged herself from Zooey's leg and was preoccupied with jumping to trigger the sensor on the automatic paper towel dispenser.

"Is she . . . ?"

"Mine? Christ, no, she's not mine. She's my sister's."

I had completely forgotten that Zooey had an older sister. She certainly acted like an only child. My relationship with Zooey is not unlike a bag of potato chips that, once the chips were freed from their bloated prison of air, is about ninety percent space and ten percent chips. It was true that I had known her for more than ten years. But within that ten years, I probably had about half as many solid hours' worth of quality interaction with her. And not unlike diet potato chips, those solid times had consistently left me feeling guilty and given me a stomachache. So I was surprised when, for the second time in our sporadic relationship, Zooey Ellis proceeded to open up that dam in her face and babble to the most unlikely of candidates: me.

The fact that Emma wasn't hers was pure coincidence. Since last we left off, Zooey had become a bit of a harlot. She had not one but two abortions, one of which resulted from a one-night stand with her best friend's boyfriend. She had gotten into drugs in Arizona, which seemed vaguely glamorous to me at first, incurring images of road trips and peyote, but significantly less so when Zooey described her abusive relationship with her dealer, who was also the assistant manager of a Whataburger. When not being smacked around or impregnated, Zooey found her "special moments" at the University of Arizona, majoring in geography.

"Is that like cartography?" I asked, wondering if there was a use for such a thing anymore. I was under the impression that the world was kind of done, that we had accepted its parameters and moved on. Like ashtrays. Or ketchup. Or bricks. These things were about as good as they were going to get.

"No," she corrected me. "It's more about maps."

There was a pause. Where was this useful education back when I was spouting theories about California's coastline-only population? We stood there smiling at Emma, using her as a visual crutch. The board game of our lives turned out to be significantly more complicated than the actual board game of Life. I made a note to myself to patent a Girl Talk for adults. You could spin the wheel, have some unprotected sex with an inappropriate partner, and your number of abortions would correspond to the birth month of the girl next to you. Let us not befriend December babies!

"Aunt Zooey, look," said Emma, who was busy pretending industrial-pink hand soap was "fairy guts."

Zooey went to collect her niece. It was time to go. The bathroom, after all, is a transient space. Not a place but a place in between. There's a reason the bathroom fixture in my apartment is host to the only lightbulb I've never had to change. People are not meant to dawdle in places like this. Besides, what more did I have to say to Zooey Ellis? The Zooey I knew and loathed was back in my suburban bedroom, her face pressed like a flower in my middle-school yearbook, where we were both living in the past and playing catch-up.

As I turned to leave, I heard a faint *ting* by our feet. The lipstick pepper spray had fallen out of my pocket and rolled back and forth between the grimy moats of tile caulk. Emma picked it up. Already trained in the lipstick arts, she immediately took the cap off. I lunged for it, but Emma retreated beneath the sinks, giggling between the corroded pipes. I crouched down.

"It's not a big deal." Zooey laughed, and as she did a piece of the old her emerged. The piece that would gleefully make you lap up water like a dog and stick plastic on your face and leave grammatically self-defeating ransom notes in your locker. And still any offense you took would be just that: something you chose to take, a fault buried deep within, a crack that began with the insecurity in your gut and ran straight up to your tear ducts. How uptight and lame I was, squatting on the bathroom floor!

"Yeah, that's pepper spray."

Zooey's eyes widened.

"Give me that, Emma," she gasped, not squatting but getting on her hands and knees like a dog on a grimy bathroom floor, grasping at this miniature version of herself.

"That's not a toy."

An Abbreviated
Catalog of Tongues

Name something."

These are the two words that invariably leave my mouth when the subject of house pets arises. Which it does, and quite often, and not without a twinge of competition. I'll see your gerbil and raise you a hamster. I'll see your bunny and raise you a ferret. I'll see your Burmese python and run. To what end this conversation is aiming, I have no idea. It would seem the winner is just one can of Resolve and a "Hang in there!" poster away from *Grey Gardens*. But I feel compelled to participate in the game anyway. So long as I don't play with people who grew up on ostrich farms. I can't compete with an ostrich. Nothing beats an ostrich.

From the day I arrived on this earth to the day I left for college, my parents lived by the philosophy that it was better to have pooped and scooped than never to have pooped at all. They acted as both host and executioner to just about every animal they could squeeze through the front door.

In junior high, when my sister began to question the long-term viability of her first steady boyfriend, she noted that he lived in a house with six siblings and no pets.

"Not even a sea monkey?"

"Not even," she said, as if his parents were sending him to school shoeless, crack cocaine in the lunchbox.

"But how does that work?"

"I guess their family just forms attachments to each other."

"Sounds awful."

How could she trust a man with no pets? How else does one learn about love and sympathy, about death and biology? Pets were such an integral part of our childhoods. Even those who had come and gone before I was alive were immortalized in my sister's scrapbook, a dog skull and crossbones on the cover. They were as legendary to me as historical figures.

To say our family had a lot of pets when I was growing up is an understatement. A lot of the people had a lot of pets a lot of the time. But to say that our answering machine informed callers they had reached "the family zoo," that the bottles of animal medications outnumbered the bottles of human medications, that the local vet dedicated a collage of Polaroids to our brood, is accurate. We were not an Eau de Cat Piss house, but we were not messing around: Yes to the cat, to the dog, to the rabbit, to the guinea pig. Yes to the frog, to the spider, to the crab, to the bird. Yes to the iguana, to the turtle, to the lizard. No to the giraffe. Where the fuck would we get a giraffe?

Whatever the reason, giraffes are the universal extreme. If you claim you're packing half an ark's worth, the average person will spit back "giraffe" at the same rate they pick 7 when presented with a range of 1 through 10. No one knows why. You would think a Siberian tiger or one really pissed-off monkey could do more damage to a living room. I can only assume it has something to do with potential chandelier entanglements or the cartoonish idea of a head shooting up through the attic, munching on grandma's wedding dress. *Moths again? Nope, that's just Spotty, the thousand-pound ruminant we keep in the basement.* Or else it's the British colonial fantasy of wildlife. A *Vanity Fair* giraffe that ambled about on our "grounds." But our lives were never quite that exotic. We were just one small family. And to say that we loved our animals is not wrong, but to say that we attempted to love them is more right.

FIRST, THE FISH

A rational parental response to a nine- and a fourteen-year-old's tears shed over a dead goldfish is to stop buying goldfish. My parents decided to up the ante. They installed a four-by-four-foot saltwater fish tank in the middle of our living room.

It should be noted that although this was the 1980s, we did not live in a particularly 1980s house. The fish tank, unaccompanied by leather sofas or miniature Zen sand gardens, was severely out of place. We had no fiber-optic sculptures or splatter paint of any kind. The only neon in sight would come years later, and was actually outside the house. As a joke, my sister's friend installed a pink neon frame around the license plate of my sister's car, which lit up along with the headlights. The car was tan. It was never meant to be in such close proximity to anything so aggressively pink. But my sister developed a Fluorescent Nightingale complex toward the device. I had no such affection for the number-obscuring glow, which brought me both ridicule and a vehicle violation ticket. I was a child of the '80s but a teenager of the '90s. I spoke flannel, not glitter. When I asked my father to cut the wiring, I was met with an *Aww, but look how happy it makes her!* This identical tone would later be used in response to our house cat vigorously licking her anus on my lap.

The fish tank, however, I didn't mind. It was our one tribute to the decade, our sole acknowledgment of that impulse to capture the exotic corners of the world, shrink them down, and sell them. Instead of having vials of ash from Mount St. Helens and chunks of the Berlin Wall, we had clown fish, sea anemones, starfish, tiger fish, tangs, and that disc-shaped yellow fish I can never remember the name of. Oh, and sea horses. The mortality rate among sea horses is not to be believed. Because the difference between a dead sea horse and a living sea horse is imperceptible, selling dead sea horses would make a very good pet store scam.

Certainly it would have been better than what our local pet store was actually doing. Which was putting chemical drops into the tanks of transparent fish to knock them out and painting hot-pink and -blue stripes on their unconscious bodies. Unless you are Assyrian, which I doubt you are, you are not allowed to tattoo, paint, or pierce your animals. This includes people who dress their pets up for Halloween. Stuffed reindeer antlers are a gateway drug. Before you know it, you'll be roofie-ing your rabbits just to glue extra cotton to their butts, watching the confusion unfold once they regain consciousness. You are a sick, sick person.

"We can do your initials if you want," the pet store guy offered.

We had just gotten the tank, and I was still learning about fish. It was an educational tool and a time-suck in one. I grimaced at the engraving proposition. They didn't have to anesthetize the roses in *Alice's Adventures in Wonderland* to paint them. That's because they were plants. And fictional. And *plants*.

My father was across the tank showroom with the owner, enmeshed in a conversation about the hazards of introducing a blowfish to a narrow tank.

"No, thank you," I said, turning to face the dye-smeared fish. They were clear from gill to gill except for their bold artificial stripes. If you blurred your eyes, the effect was a tank full of floating computer cursors.

The pet store guy shrugged, mildly offended.

"My middle name starts with a *G*," I explained.

I could barely write a cursive *G* on paper. It seemed an especially cruel letter to inflict on a fish.

When my father returned, he had a bag of goldfish in his hand. The fish wavered in size as they swam between the corners of the bag. Unlike the fat gold balls that perished in our tiny bedroom tanks, these were thin and frantic. And many. There were sold by the dozen. I knew that the salt-water tank had been more of a financial commitment than my parents had bargained for, but fish-by-the-yard seemed like a far cry from a miniature shark.

"They're feeder fish," my father said.

This seemed wrong. Surely this was an unfortunate nickname, but they had real names, like our other fish. If I were a tiger fish, I would tease a fish called "feeder" merci-lessly. Although if I were a clown fish, I'd probably keep my mouth shut.

"For what?"

"For him." My father stepped aside. The pet store owner appeared with a portable tank. Inside was a gray stingray, pushing himself back and forth from the edges like a broken Frisbee.

Herb. Herb was the worst stingray ever.

Herb hung out unviciously at the bottom of the tank, making the sea horses look caffeinated. He was a depressive, colored a bit like a black-and-white cookie, with about the same capacity for free will. And he shed. Little gray bits of him became trapped in the sea anemones. We'd have been better off with a dress-eating giraffe. Herb was just biding his time until that great journey to the surface. If he had any inclination toward appearing majestic or graceful, he kept it to himself. His only activity was to eat, which he did rarely. Though it was a sight to behold if you happened to be in the room for it.

In the wild, stingrays will corner their prey against a piece of coral or a slab of rock. But Herb insisted on trapping the feeder fish against the glass of the tank and slurping them up through the hole in his belly while two dumbstruck little girls stood agape in their pajamas, watching nature unfold. Otherwise, he played dead at an Oscar-worthy level. One day his performance was so convincing, I thought he had willed himself to die just by staying still for too long. I went running to get my sister so that she could confirm rigor-ray-tis. Of course by then she had grown bored of Herb and, by association, me. She spent more and more time away from the house, off in some cavernous movie theater or food court with her friends. Or with her petless wonder of a boyfriend. I grabbed a thin gold necklace from her room and lowered it into the tank in an attempt to rouse the patient. More than waking him, I wanted him to become the graceful ribbon of the sea that was his destiny. My sister had let me stay up to watch *The Abyss* the last time she babysat. I knew how this thing was supposed to move.

I dangled the necklace into the deep, probing for life. This expedition continued for a good four seconds before I dropped it. The chain landed on a piece of salmon coral. The mineral balance of saltwater tanks is fragile. This is the reason the tank is not to be found in my parents' home right now. After a few years, they would tire of cleaning it, of checking the thermometers, and especially of forgetting to check the thermometers. They would figure out cheaper ways for their two girls to bond. Like television. And that eventually, we'd bond ourselves with the lending of the driver's licenses for the buying of the beer and the not telling on of the older one when she lit the garage on fire trying to smoke weed out of a Coke can.

But this was before that. The saltwater tank was pretty much it. So I scurried out of the family room to the kitchen, where I found salad tongs long enough to retrieve the necklace. But by the time I got back, the necklace had vanished. I scanned for it, tongs frozen above the surface, ready to act. It wasn't in the coral or the gravel or the corner of the glass. It wasn't one of my sister's favorites, but I worried she might notice it missing from her collection. I combed through the gravel with the tongs. I could sense Herb staring

at me, judging me through his invisible eyes, located somewhere above his turgid tummy. He was dead by midnight.

THE HAMSTER AND THE TURTLE

The hamster rarely acts alone. Similar-caliber animals tend
to be present in a house if there's a hamster upstairs. Our
hamster, for instance, was accompanied by a turtle. My parents liked the idea of these two animals, so disparate in texture and temperament but tallied on the same receipt. Kind
of like their children. Or the tortoise and the hare.

My sister named her turtle Fred. Because I'd use any
means possible to get closer to her, I named my hamster
Ginger. Plus, it worked with her coloring. Fred and Ginger were impulse pets, twin symbols of our parents' good
intentions gone wrong. They were acquired during one of
those record-skipping moments in which people who have
two children still manage to mix up their spawn. Upon
meeting us, you would know that I am the turtle person
and my sister is the hamster person. You would not be
required to give birth to us to gain this insight. My sister
is not especially hyper, and I am not especially slothful,
although, truth be told, we're a little of both those things.
However, if there were such a thing as the Sign of the Hamster, I would not be born under it.

I used Ginger to gain access to my sister's room, because

Ginger was a hell of a lot more interesting to her than Fred was. My sister bonded with that tailless rat. I would put the plump beast in Barbie's Corvette and have her "drive" the car down the carpeted highway and into my sister's room. Hamster feet are quite thin, like miniature chicken feet. They're hairless and flexible, so that if you force one to grab a plastic steering wheel at ten and two, it looks freakishly realistic. If you are ever presented with the opportunity, I suggest you take it.

But caring for Ginger wasn't worth the price of admission to my sister's room. I was the one who had to live with Ginger, but I was far from her ideal keeper. The wheel in her cage squeaked in circles all night long. When she gave that a rest, she'd start in on the metal ball of her water feeder. Once I sneaked down to the liquor cabinet and put a couple of drops of vodka in her water in an ineffective attempt to sedate her. More than once I covered her soiled wood chips with a layer of fresh ones.

Meanwhile, I kept a watchful eye out for Fred, inquiring about the frequency of his feedings and the clarity of his water.

"Do you think you should change it?"

"It's supposed to get a little disgusting," my sister would say, rescuing Ginger from the driver's seat.

And she was right. But when the muck is so clouded you mistake a rock for your pet, you're abusing the system.

I don't know why we didn't switch pets. Maybe we didn't want to hurt our parents' feelings. Maybe we didn't understand our parents. It was probably because of a deference I had toward my sister. Some animals have a maturity stamp, and I believe she felt it was wrong for her to own a hamster at her age. Playing with a hamster was like playing with a plastic recorder or a little sister. I didn't see why she would feel this way. Ginger was the only one of us to drink *and* get behind the wheel of a vehicle.

Fred and Ginger died on the exact same day. Caught in star-crossed pet affection, my sister found Ginger, and I found Fred. Sad as I was for Fred, I will say that a dead turtle is easier on the eyes than a dead hamster. Their joint deaths enabled us to mourn at the dinner table under the guise of the other pet's passing. We could air our grief out in the open as neither of their habitats had been aired out when they were alive. When we dragged ourselves upstairs after dinner, my sister cried. Then I cried. Then she kicked me out of her room.

THE DOG

During my formative teen years, my father's favorite thing in the world was to joke around with visitors and guests about our blind dog. He'd claim that after the guest left, he was going to rearrange the furniture just to see what happened. Turn the ottoman a few degrees and see how she fared. The dog panted on the edge of the sofa, her coffee eyes clouded white, as if someone had dropped a dollop of cream in each and forgotten to stir. A purebred bichon frise, the dog had sudden-onset cataracts at three months. As if her being inbred wasn't enough to put a dent in my affections, I cursed her for her genetic distance from a normal-sized canine. I lamented our inability to "get a real dog." I had seen scrapbook pictures of a lovable golden retriever and a standard poodle towering over me as an infant. What happened to their ilk? Bichon frises are dogs for cat people. They won't fit in a purse, but they will fit in a beach bag, which is philosophically the same thing.

In the winter, we'd let her play in the snow. We made this mistake every year. And every year she blended in so perfectly, we lost track of her just as she'd lost track of us.

How many preteen girls in America hate their dogs? It was unnatural. Should I also be pouring salt on slugs and tearing the wings off moths? I did not want to grow up to become a sociopath. So I tried to love the dog as best I could. When that failed, I could always fall back on the fact that she was never supposed to be mine.

"A puppy" had been my sister's request. Yet the feeding and walking of this thing fell to me. Did this make it okay when I ignored her whimpers for foul-scented soft food and gave her dry instead? Did it make it okay for me to let her off the leash to go play in the street before school each morning? Did it make it okay when I'd forget to open the screen door, causing her to jump straight into it like a bird? Probably not.

"It's not her fault," my mother would say, slyly gesturing at the dog's eyes, as if she could see through them.

"I don't hate her because she's blind," I'd argue. "I hate her because of who she is."

"You said a mouthful there, kiddo," said my dad, handing me the pooper-scooper.

The bichon was a long-standing wish of my sister's, granted just in time for her to leave for college, as was the habit with my parents. By the time you'd sufficiently hinted at something (a minimum of two years was generally required for an inanimate object, four for a living one), you had outgrown it. This led to several instances of my father providing a scavenger hunt of clues around the house, culminating in the formerly desired gifts. My mother must have feared she'd raised two rather stupid children, as the clues would have been obvious were they better timed. Instead, I'd open a note that said something like "You're the most stable person I know!" hinting at the My Little Pony dream house I'd begged for when I was eight. Or my sister would tear open the wrapping around a can of tennis balls, indicating the purchase of tickets to a sporting event in which she had shown no recent interest. She'd crack the can open, searching for a more tailored clue, only to recoil at the scent. Then she'd hand the balls to me—my parents' actual tennis-playing child. Ever the mastermind behind this process, my father would grin with anticipation. And we were compelled to reciprocate the expression as a placeholder while we scoured our brains for the answer, eyes as glazed over and useless as the dog's.

THE BIRDS

You wouldn't think it would be so hard to keep tabs on the birds, their living in a cage as they did. But they came and went so quickly, and for so many years. When I'd uncover them to let the light in each morning, I'd often forget who it was I was waking up. My father went through bird phases: parakeets and canaries, then cockatiels and lovebirds. He bought two lovebirds, though apparently they're quite egotistical by nature. One lovebird + one mirror = a happy bird experience. Meanwhile, rainbow finches filled the time and space between. They were all incredibly fragile creatures. I came to look on their expected life spans as I would later look on home maintenance products like hair dye and waxing kits. "Up to eight weeks" really means "two and a half weeks if you're lucky."

After my sister left for college, I became depressed on behalf of the birds. I was convinced they lived such short lives because they were forbidden to fly. Just like me, a teenager who felt she would surely die like this, trapped alone with *these people* in *this house*. I had decided that everything about my life was tepid, so naturally my vote for our next bird was a giant cockatoo or a parrot or something you could keep on a wooden pole and eccentrically bequeath. I wanted one of these birds despite being petrified of their beaks. Is it such a good idea to purchase an animal whose face is the basis for can openers? It didn't matter, anyway. Giant cockatoos were too expensive, especially given our track record of killing the cheaper models. Plus, they talked back. I wondered what language a cockatoo would regurgitate if it lived in our house. Can a bird imitate the sound of a bedroom door slamming?

My sister had driven home after her freshman year just in time to see the final finches go.

"What's happening to them?"

"Isn't it obvious?" I said. "They're dying of boredom."

In truth, it hadn't occurred to me that their deaths could be related. If there was a problem, surely it lay with us and not the birds. She scooped up their lifeless bodies with dishtowels and put them in a shoe box.

"Grab the cage," she instructed. College girl, problem solver.

A man in a Bird World vest (*Bird World: because a lot is riding on your talons!*) accepted our shoe box without opening it and looked suspiciously at the cage. He got out a Q-tip and ran the cotton head along the wires. Apparently, the cage was covered in a poisonous, scentless, invisible mold. The birds weren't fragile or suicidal; we had been escorting them to their deaths. It was all our fault after all.

"We're bird Nazis," I said as I got back into the car, buried my head in my hands, and started to cry.

"They're like pigeons," said my sister. "It's not like we're murdering African grays. Honestly, you were going to outgrow them soon, anyway."

"I know! But . . ." I continued to bawl.

"Hey." She put her arm around me and rubbed my shoulder. "Why don't you come visit me at school?"

"Okay"—I sniffed—"maybe I will."

THE SQUIRREL

There was an albino squirrel that lived on our property. We'd toss him the pistachio nuts we couldn't open. One evening my father spotted this pouffy flash of white violently tearing the bark off a hickory tree. He picked up a rock, thinking he'd throw it into the branches and scare the animal away. The squirrel turned around, caught the rock in its mouth, slammed its little head against the tree, fell down, and died.

FINALLY, THE CATS

Pick a number between 1 and 10.

That's how many cats we had. Though not all at once. There was the Siamese that meowed like a baby. The tortoiseshell that had worms. The prissy Persian that ran from impending feet. I always felt sorry for the Persian and its overly aligned features. To have a face that flat, to have no profile to speak of, is to never be able to send your nose into a situation ahead of you. There is no preliminary exploration of a stranger's hand or a new pair of sneakers. You just have to go for it, get your whole head in there at once. Our prissy Persian was, to my mind, excessively judicious in these matters. So much unlike our fourth cat, who had no reservations about smelling anything ever.

A fearless black brute, Bucky led a pack of raccoons. We'd see him traipsing through the backyard at night with an honest-to-God pack of raccoons in V formation behind him. Like geese. My father built Bucky a cat-sized wooden shed outside, and for fifteen years he and the raccoons would change shifts at dawn. It was a point of pride for my father that our cat selflessly recognized the raccoons' need for shelter. Cats are dilettantes of the nocturnal world, compared to raccoons. Although my sister and I were taught not to go near the shed during the day, since it was essentially Nap Time for Rabies.

Bucky was something else. My mother had dozed off one summer afternoon and my sister and I woke her, telling her that the cat—who left modest presents of dead mice on the doorstep—had really outdone himself.

"Mommy." My sister shook my mother's shoulder. "Bucky killed an eagle."

"It's a pigeon." My mother spoke to the interior of the bed. "Dad will take care of it later."

"Mommy!" My sister shook again. "Bucky killed an eagle!"

I nodded. I had seen the eagle in question.

Finally roused, my mother allowed herself to be escorted downstairs by two small hands that flanked her like training wheels. When she opened the front door, there it was. Bucky had not, in fact, killed an eagle. What he had done was tear the heart out of an adult hawk with a wingspan that exceeded the width of our doormat. We had a family meeting. Rather than put the ASPCA on speed-dial, we put a small bell on the cat's collar. Which had no effect whatsoever. He just stalked more methodically.

Two days before he died, Bucky cornered a tiny stray kitten on our porch, and we took it in. Now, my parents are not big believers in God. Or, rather, they believe in him partially. Which is tricky. It's like being kind of pregnant or only mostly dead. You're either in or you're out. The only time they evoked God with any certainty was when speaking of how Bucky *knew* he was dying and didn't want us to be lonely. So Bucky and God put their heads together and placed this precious kitten in the right place at the right time. At the vet's suggestion, my parents filled latex gloves with kitten formula and let her drink from the fingers. My father watched over the new kitten as if she were the Virgin Mary in a potato chip.

This zealous logic lasted about a week. They were only delaying the inevitable. They were in mourning for our beloved cat and couldn't be bothered reconstructing their affections with a new kitten. God or no God. My father tore down the shed and retired the bell. *The stars are not wanted now: put out every one; / Pack up the moon and dismantle the sun.* My parents scratched the kitten's ears out of habit. If it's possible to play with yarn in a sullen fashion, they did it. When she performed some amusing kitten antic, they cooed the way Hollywood producers laugh—by saying "That's funny" instead of actually laughing. This defeatist attitude reached its nadir with the naming of the kitten.

"We're calling her Kitty Kitty," said my mother, in a totally monotone I-don't-give-a-shit-about-this-animal voice.

"You can't do that," my sister and I protested.

"But that's what she responds to," said my father.

And that we couldn't argue with. My sister had been out

of the house for years, and I was off to college in a matter of months. *Someone* had to come when called.

So we kept quiet, both of us privately knowing that a cat with a name like that wouldn't live past a year at the outside.

It didn't help matters that Kitty Kitty had a thing for cars. Not only did she possess a quarter of Bucky's yard smarts, she seemed not to have been raised by cats at all. By auto mechanics, maybe. When she wasn't plowing headfirst into the garage door, she'd hop onto the trunk of any car that came up the driveway. She was manning a one-pussy drive-through safari. She'd chase cars down the road, dense as a Dalmatian prancing after a fire truck.

How, we wondered, did we come to be in possession of such a suicidal animal? Maybe she was not suicidal at all but simply running after these strange vehicles as if to say, "Take me with you!" Could she sense our ambivalence? Was it that obvious? A lifetime of pet affection had worn us down. All those different cans and bags of food! The different sizes and consistencies of waste pellets! The jingling and the squeaking and the neediness! The tongues alone. Paper-thin lizard tongues that looked like they'd been clipped with shirring scissors, dry bird tongues, humid dog tongues, tiny rabbit tongues, rough cat tongues that loved you by accident if you got in the way of a bath.

A year to the day after we took in the kitten, my mother was backing out of the garage when she heard an unnaturally high-pitched meow. This time I was the one home from college for the weekend. I pulled into the driveway and she was waiting for me, looking sullen. The cat had not hopped on my hood.

"You killed her. Didn't you?" I said. I didn't have to ask how it happened.

"I'm sorry." She nodded.

"Sure." I sat next to my mother on our front steps. "You're not even sad."

"I'm a little sad."

"Are not. You killed our cat today—show some remorse, woman!"

"Actually"—she covered her mouth—"I killed her yesterday."

"I told you guys you never should have named her that."

THE END

Those pets who weren't flushed down the toilet or euthanized by the vet (oddly, a licensed veterinarian will not just hand over a dead iguana in a bag) got buried in the backyard. But not in the way most house pets get buried in the backyard. My father puts the animals in Tupperware. Each creature is buried in an aptly sized container that has been duct-taped into a silver blob. This is meant to ensure that their eternal slumber, along with the newly seeded lawn, remains undisturbed by other animals. But when I imagine the rounded plastic pools of rotting bones and gas, I have to ask: Who is this really helping? Not us when we imagine it. Not the animals that are buried in a manner that flies in the face of Mother Nature.

Instead of asking, we just accept it. My sister says this is part of becoming an adult, accepting our parents' illogical behaviors just as they used to accept ours. The Tupperware coffins are but one of my father's many questionable schemes. Walk into any room of his home and you will spend an inordinate amount of time slapping the wall, trying to turn the lights on, because a switch so high-tech you have to blow on it has just been installed. Pour yourself a glass of water from the kitchen sink and see if one of the jiggered spray settings doesn't soak your shirt.

My sister was at school and I went to the movies the night Kitty Kitty was buried. My mother, not guilty but ambivalent, wanted no part of it. I felt like we were missing something as a family. Despite her low rung on the ladder of favorites, Kitty Kitty held the distinction of Last of the Childhood Pets. I thought it might be good to have a real funeral. Not good enough to miss out on a trip to the movies, but just enough to think about it in general.

"There's a joke about Jewish holidays," one of us would begin, "that each holiday has the same theme. And that theme is: *They tried to kill us. We lived. Let's drink*. Well, as we look around at our pets today, we think: *We tried to love them. They died. Let's bury them.*"

Then we'd stand around a headstone and drink some nice beer and listen to the crickets. We'd have a dinner outside that involved asparagus, because for some reason asparagus always gets in there. And my father would raise his bottle and toast to the many tongues that supported us throughout the years.

In reality, it was just a man alone with his Tupperware collection of dead animals. See him there, in the dirt, digging at dusk. A shovel put back in the garage, a light switch brutally smacked, an alarm clock mistakenly set for p.m. so that the buttons have to be clicked all the way around again. Behind all our great pets—even behind all our mediocre pets—is the man who bought and buried them. These dead animals are so sad. They are the only things we buy and bury with the intention of covering them up for good. Buried treasure, flower bulbs, umbrellas in the sand: they're all meant to come back up. But with dead pets, you just have to say good-bye, cut your losses, and start over. I used to know the location of every plastic coffin in the dirt, but I haven't gone back there in such a long time.

Le Paris!

It's incredibly difficult to get yourself banished from a city. A country is not so tough. There are words for that on both sides of the border. *Emigrate. Defect. Deport.* But when New Yorkers use those words to explain their residency here, what they really mean is that they packed their bags and got on a plane and it meant more to them than it did to anyone else. No one stopped them. No one checked their papers in Hoboken. No one kept them in quarantine in Queens. No one earns a living being stationed at the Lincoln Tunnel and scowling. At least not technically, they don't. Because as it is with most cities, this one is porous. We absorb the new and sweat out the old and put about as much conscious effort into it as we do into actually sweating. Once you're in, you really have to get creative to be pushed back out.

It's not so tough to get yourself banished from a person's apartment. Smoke in the freshly painted bathroom. Feed the dog chocolate. Ask the hosts if they think it's weird that their two-year-old hasn't started talking yet. The door shuts, the bolt locks, the whispers commence, and your passport to game night gets revoked faster than you can say "baby fish mouth." But in order to get bounced from a city, that place in between, you have to break the public transit system. Or execute some very specific offense on par with killing your young lover's cousin in a vicious street fight in Verona. Or run for office.

I didn't do any of those things to Paris. I loved Paris. Which is why it's especially painful knowing that, like a boarding school reject, I will not be "asked back" anytime soon. Though I was not formally banished, Paris has made it clear that it would prefer to continue on in its Frenchness *sans moi*. To sweat me out. Imagine what it is to be rejected by the most sophisticated and casually stunning place in the world. A place filled with the highest percentage of women on the planet able to pull off chinchilla wraps with jeans. To not be welcome in the City of Love is tantamount to being rejected by love itself. Why couldn't I have gotten thrown out of Akron, Ohio, City of Rubber?

MY FRIEND LOUISE HAD SUBLET AN APARTMENT IN Paris for a month, so I found the cheapest red-eye possible and booked my flight. Because this is what you do when your friend calls from Paris to tell you how wonderful the very worst of everything is over there. You go out and buy an international adapter plug kit, lay the plug heads on your bed, and stare at the beveled prongs. You feel the sudden urge to travel sixteen hours to Fiji just to plug something in. A toaster, maybe. But Fiji, she will have to wait. Paris is calling! The entire city is spinning with sophistication, like a child's top. The Eiffel Tower is the handle.

Having just successfully deplaned, I was already trying on the Parisian version of myself. This version of my personhood was distinctly laid-back. Sometimes forcefully, if the situation required it. *What? No, honestly, take this taxi. You were here first in spirit.* Laid-back Me was sewn to my heels, a shadow with its own motivations and interests. A silhouette with a joint in one hand, a package of Ding Dongs in the other, and bunny slippers on its feet. Not that the shadow wasn't adaptable. That was part of the deal. If I had gone to Montana, I would have been laid-back and prone to liking horses. If I had gone to Tokyo, I would have been laid-back and unfazed by pornographic comic books and confounding soft-drink packaging. If I had gone to Rome, I would have done as they do. Now I had returned to Paris to be laid-back and—who knew what? *The shadow knows.* Consume unseemly quantities of macaroons, maybe.

This laid-back version of me decided to surprise Louise by navigating public transport from the airport to her apartment. Having been to Paris once before, I had a vague sense of its layout. In New York, I couldn't find my way out of a paper bag. Or, more accurately, a used paper bag. I forgot the paths to the same locations no sooner than I had found them. But the Parisian streets were generous with me, rewarding my instinct to veer left or turn right with the correct street names drilled to the walls of each corner. When I located Louise's address, I realized she was right: the worst of the worst here looks a lot like the best of our best. Everything about the building was perfect, right down to the doors—sturdy but worn wooden twins that earned their distress. Like a great pair of jeans. I exchanged grins with a woman who entered the building ahead of me. This would be a double surprise. Any closer and Louise would wake up with me sitting creepily at the end of her bed, watching her sleep.

"*Bonjour*, Louise," I'd say, all *Hello, Clarice*.

Maybe just inside the door was far enough.

The woman held the door. I was still mute with embarrassment, my tongue like the neck of a turtle retracted in the shell of my face. I speak "get by" French. Also known as "*bicyclette rouge* French" to anyone who's ever cracked open a blue, white, and red textbook. *Est-ce que vous avez une bicyclette rouge? Oui, ici est ma bicyclette rouge.* If McGraw-Hill is to be believed, red bicycles are government-issued in France. Also, everyone in France is *très fatigué* all the time, likely from their late nights buttering bread and sending telegrams.

The woman allowed me to follow her, rolling my suit-case clumsily over the cobblestone of the courtyard. When she slid a key into a door on the first floor, she glanced back over her shoulder and smiled again, this time more furtively, which I translated to mean "You gonna be okay out here?" but which probably meant something along the lines of "Please don't kill my family with whatever's in that bag." I sat on my suitcase and called Louise, somewhat horrified by the expensive trip the signal took, ricocheting between hemispheres.

"Well, hello there," I said, anxious to surprise her with my presence not at the *métro* stop, as planned, but delivered right to her front door. *Quel service!*

"Guess where I am."

"At the metro stop?"

"*Non!* In your courtyard."

"What?"

"In your courtyard?"

I didn't understand why she couldn't get on board with my enthusiasm. I had saved her much clunking up metro steps with an obvious fellow tourist, and this allowed her another day of native make-believe. One's own touristicity is easily submerged—watch what you put on your feet, lose the raincoat, try not to look up so much—but *two* tourists are a different story. It's the same principle that allows one to dart like a pixilated frog across oncoming traffic when alone but forces one to wait for a blinking light when with a group, watching old ladies with walkers and mothers with strollers dart past. It's why spies don't have friends and serial killers don't start book clubs. There is no safety in numbers.

"That's impossible," said Louise, waking up.

"Well"—I gave my haughtiest chuckle—"the laws of time and space would beg to differ."

"I don't have a courtyard."

In a moment of temporary dyslexia, Louise had e-mailed me the wrong address. Worse, she couldn't recall her own address. *This is not a problem!* said my laid-back-ness, as it waited for Louise to go downstairs and consult her front door. But when I went to leave I discovered that the giant doors to the street had locked behind me. The metal knobs refused to turn, despite my repeated attempts to convince them. I shook them, imagining how futile a couple of vibrating doors on a bustling Parisian avenue appeared from the other side. I went back into the courtyard, but there were no signs of life, just a few curtains blowing in the open windows above and some very annoying birds. It was nine a.m. I glanced at the door on the first floor. *This is not a problem!* said my laid-back self. Louise got back on the phone, at which point I explained that I was being held hostage by this strange building.

"Okay," she said. "I'm coming to find you."

I didn't know how French blocks worked. I knew only that I was somewhere on a street as long as Broadway and the address had been botched using four digits. I had some time. The first pangs of jet lag washed over me. Sometimes the worst of the worst is actually the worst. Tired of fiddling with the lock, I stepped back and roundhouse kicked it for my own amusement. I did this at the exact right angle to set off the security alarm. Like its cousin, the ambulance siren, this alarm blared in a French accent—singsongy and oddly un-urgent. But it echoed like a bitch.

This is not a problem! said my laid-back-ness. I needed to unstitch this slacker shadow before I punched it.

"For who are you *cherch*ing?" said an elderly Frenchman who appeared from absolutely nowhere. He was angry and quasi-bilingual. He spoke while charging at me and tightening his bathrobe. The rough hair springing from his ears was just long enough to allow for mobility, and it waved with his marching. I looked over his shoulder, searching for a hallway or a stairwell or a dumbwaiter. Right now I was *cherch*ing for any possible Crazy French Dude point of origin.

"You *frenchfrenchfrench* idiot. I get the *frenchfrenchfrench* police!"

"*Zut,*" I said, hands in the air. Are you even allowed to threaten to call the police in your bathrobe anymore?

"*Je suis très desolé.*"

That's another thing about *bicyclette rouge* French. No one in France ever finds himself moderately hungry or reasonably happy. They are always very everything.

"*Mais,*" I continued, as he eyed my suitcase stuffed

with hypothetically stolen goods, *"je pense que j'ai le mal building."*

Because I could not think of the word for "wrong," I used the word for "bad." Ah, influency, recipe for extremes. I had broken into this gentlemen's building to insult it. Which, come to think of it, seemed like something a French robber would do.

Perhaps I had inadvertently stumbled on the word "cocksucker" as well, because then came a torrent of French followed by a mercifully dry spitting gesture. The veins of French vocabulary may run thin with a low word count, but they know how to bleed. I have reason to believe I was called a squirrel at one point. But he may also have been calling me a school. I cocked my head at him. Had the use of "school" as a verb crossed continents? And would this man, with his astonishingly wiry nose hair, be familiar with it? One thing was certain: I was being schooled, run over like a half-dead squirrel. Bump, bump.

"S'il vous plaît," I reasoned with him through the sound of the siren, *"pas de polizia. Je suis normale!"*

"Normale?"

"Ish."

"D'accord. Go, go, go," he said in English, shoving me aside to perform a series of doorknob twists befitting a Rubik's Cube.

I peeked outside, hesitant as a cat to leave her cage at the vet's office. Louise was not there yet. When she finally did arrive, I was sitting on my suitcase, ignoring the coolly revolted glares of people passing by and playing with a zipper. My arms extended, I buried my head in my elbows.

"I feel like I should give you money." Louise bent down and hugged me.

"That's so weird." I looked up. "I also feel like you should give me money."

Not being the most reliable navigator, I would get Louise lost many times in the coming days. After a while, it was as much her fault as it was mine for deciding to follow me. But I couldn't blame her. Looking at a map requires an activation of concentration even if you don't have spatial-relations issues, the same way cooking raw chicken requires an activation of "let's just get through this part" even if you're not a vegetarian. Because we were staying in the Marais, a neighborhood defined by narrow sidewalks and independent shops and very small cups of coffee, neither of us minded the winding routes home. Nothing seemed to take that long, and when it did, we didn't care: we were in Paris. If we swung especially far off course, we'd pass the old man's building.

"Look"—Louise would point, with a shopping bag–weighted arm—"your fake apartment building."

We took pictures of it. It became our anti-landmark, how we knew we were headed in the wrong direction. And I'd look at the door and think of how thoroughly unappealing it seemed from the other side. I'd think of the last thing the old man said to me as he escorted me off his property. He gestured at the courtyard, then at me, then at the negative space of the open door.

"*Frenchfrenchfrench*," he said. "I do not *frenchfrench* think you should come to this place again."

He probably meant just the apartment building. But I took it to mean all of Paris.

AFTER THAT FIRST DAY, I AWOKE TO THE VAGUE BUT identifiable smell of cheese. The kind of cheese where if you didn't know it was cheese, you'd think someone took a crap on the metro and set it on fire. And then put it out with milk. I meandered into the kitchen to see a composition of French consumption on the table: bottles of red wine, baguettes, leeks, an entire wheel of Brie, and a jar of something that may or may not have been mayonnaise. It also may have been marshmallow fluff. I wouldn't know. The nutritional information orbited along the outermost rings of my French vocabulary.

"I think that's mayonnaise," Louise said, sneaking up behind me and cracking a chocolate croissant in half. "What's French for mayonnaise?"

"*Mayonnaise.*"

"Then what's marshmallow?"

"Presumably *marshmalleaux*."

Any word over ten letters in English is the same word in French. Fact.

"What is all this, anyway?" I said, gesturing with the jar. It was the same way I would gesture with it in a drunken stupor two nights hence, causing it to slip from my hand, fall straight out the window and onto the street, smashing into a carnage of goop and glass. Which, to our credit, the French pigeons were also at a loss to identify.

"This is the *le beauty* of *le sublet*," she cried. "Cooking!"

Louise, a key-carrying subletter, had gone on a *supermarché* sweep. She opened a plastic container of creamed fish and spread it over her second cliché-stuffed pastry.

"Are you pregnant?"

"What?"

"*Le* knocked up. Are you?"

"No." She laughed and explained her subletting enchantment. "I just like bringing groceries back to a house. With a house, even when you've powered down for the day, you're still in a kind of cultural-immersion program."

Who was I to argue? Without even trying to take in Paris, I had already slept in someone else's low bed. I had touched their funny toilet paper, opened their medicine cabinet, banged on their faucets like a monkey, and then maneuvered their low-hanging showerhead, mumbling, *What is this, Thailand?* until I resigned myself to defeat and squatted to bathe, also like a monkey.

———

THE ONE THING I WAS MOST DETERMINED TO SEE IN Paris I wasn't sure I'd be able to find again. It wasn't mobile like a boat on the Seine or perishable like a macaroon but a public fountain rooted to the ground. The problem was that I had embellished this particular fountain in my head, applied such importance to it that the contextual scenery had all but faded away. I had held the image of it like a pearl ring, loosely pronged and unscratched. It was a peaceful place—overgrown, quaint, and stone, with cigarette butts crushed into the dirt around it. But that didn't exactly narrow it down.

But then Louise began talking about the Luxembourg Gardens. A place, I pointedly explained, where I wanted my ashes scattered one day.

"You should know this," I said, as we walked through the front gates, "so in case I die tomorrow, it's on you to pipe up."

I felt destined for it the way teenagers feel destined for inanimate objects and public spaces. *The walls of this museum know I'm special. No one understands me but this coffee mug.* I also had a fantasy about my descendants—grown, sophisticated, lovely descendants—easing their jetpacks onto the garden grounds on their way to colonize Uranus, commenting on the striking difference between this decrepit fountain crafted from earth matter and their all-white space cars made of microelectric essence. Upon seeing my final resting place, they would be reminded of their humanity and the connective thread between my ashes and the freeze-dried meat pies they ate for breakfast.

This, as it turns out, was a bust. The fountain is not quaint. Nor is its existence much of a mystery, given the fact that it is *the* fountain in the Luxembourg Gardens, measuring 8.9 million meters tall by 9.8 million meters wide and ladled with statues of historical figures and saints and curls of concrete. It had started to rain. We snapped open our shared umbrella and stood at the base. Tourists took photographs and consulted their guidebooks to confirm what they were seeing.

"Wow," Louise offered. "Think much of yourself?"

"I don't remember it being this . . . grand."

"I see gargoyles."

"It was more modest the last time."

The fountain was, as most fountains are, symbolic of something else. This one was symbolic of a larger problem I seemed to be having with Paris. My brain had misfiled the entire city, and instead of remembering it from small to big, like a stuffed animal that seems huge when you're a child and stuffed animal–sized when it's being sold at a tag sale, I remembered it from big to small. Paris ran backward. If I thought a monument or a creperie was two streets away, it was two miles away. If I thought a street looked familiar, I was wrong.

Louise read the history-explaining plaque.

"Are you even allowed to have your ashes scattered in a public fountain?"

"It's a body of water."

"It's practically stagnant," she said, pointing to the low-pressure streams meekly pouring from the Bastille-era plumbing.

"Shouldn't you just get buried, anyway? I thought Jews didn't believe in cremation."

I scoffed.

"What does this mean, 'believe in'? Makes it sound like we're living in caves and don't think it exists. Like we're all, 'Oh, fire, what's that? Is something burning? Man, this knish looks like a wheel, except I don't have that reference because *I don't know what a wheel is.*'"

"So you know what I mean, then."

I stared at the watery muck. "I want to get down and dirty with the pennies and the algae."

The truth was, I knew it didn't matter how my corporeal being was disposed of. Bury me, freeze me, deep-fry me like a Mars bar, send me to a giant corporate building with a giant corporate sign that reads SCIENCE. Nothing I did in this life would have any bearing on the path I took in the next one. I had sealed my fate ten years prior, during my first Parisian excursion. Sealed it and spat on it and locked it in, as if trapped behind a Parisian apartment door. I never did have much of a sense of direction, but I knew that when I died, I would not be going north.

MY FRIEND EMILY AND I WERE BACKPACKING AROUND Europe together in a lopsided horseshoe path that began in Spain and would end in Turkey. More than any other destination, both of us were eager to reach Paris. How could we not be?

A. Paris is awesome, and we could sense its awesomeness in advance.

B. Emily wanted to see Notre Dame before she died.

C. *Somebody* had misread the train schedule leaving Barcelona, thus resulting in an Alps-obscuring overnight train trip in which we woke up in Geneva, Switzerland, and proceeded to get into a massive fight at a train station café, which culminated in my saying something about overrated chocolate, looping my arms into my backpack, and storming out of said station to wander the streets of Geneva, thinking it would be less trouble to spend the rest of my life in a Swiss bus shelter than to sort out the next southbound train.

When I eventually returned, Emily was gone. I thought perhaps she had gone back to Spain. I wouldn't have blamed her. The weather was more pleasant in Barcelona, as was our friendship. But when I reached the appropriate platform, there she was, chin in hand, sitting on her own overstuffed backpack as if it were a giant mushroom. I plopped down next to her.

"I'm sorry," I said, which in retrospect was the right thing to say when you abandon someone in a foreign country with no sign of returning. But which I probably didn't mean at the time. Fatigue had rendered me impervious to Switzerland's neutrality vibes. Emily unstuck her hand, hung her head, and spoke to the platform.

"I tried to buy a bagel, but they won't accept French francs. I offered them fifty francs for a bagel."

"That's just sad."

"Isn't it?" she said, looking up and smiling at me. "How can we have this much difficulty getting to Paris? What would happen to us in Bogotá?"

"We'd sell our bodies to the night in exchange for cocaine and corn on sticks."

"That sounds nice."

Since we arrived a day late, the beds in our hostel of choice had been filled by a pair of German lesbian equestrians. They were in town for a convention, though we couldn't say if it was for Germans or lesbians or equestrians. Either way, we didn't put up a fight. Instead, we wandered the streets, checking into the cheapest one-fifth-of-a-star hotel we could find. Located kind of near Les Halles, it was a hotel only in the sense that a lot of people who didn't live there slept there at night. Or, rather, during the day. Like raccoons.

Hygienic hostels and grimy hotels are a little like employees in a large corporation. When graduating from entry-level, there's a gap of time in which you are no longer an assistant and thus stop receiving overtime. Your salary actually decreases. Your quality of life was better before the upgrade. Sitting in this "hotel" on a partially upholstered bench with wool protruding from the edges was like a demotion, with Emily and me doing twice the grunt work for half the perks.

"Do you think they have the Internet?" She straightened up.

"No, I don't think they have the Internet."

Meanwhile, the manager sat in a bulletproof booth and dug through a drawer of keys. I think if he had escorted us anywhere but a lit hallway, we would have run.

"Look at that." I tapped Emily on the arm and gestured toward a completely naked man down the hall. His puckered slabs of fat folded on top of one another as he bent down to feed two less judgmental cats.

I am a firm believer in not letting disgusting things be witnessed alone. Once, as I watched an old cockroach crawl across the back of my living room sofa, I called my

squeamish roommate to tell her the precise measurements
and trajectory of the roach. If I had to continue living in
our apartment knowing where it had been, I was taking her
down with me.

When we got to our room, I shut the sliding lock behind
us, and Emily propped a desk chair beneath the doorknob, a
move I was pretty sure both of us had seen only in fictional
form. There was a dried bar of used soap and a child's dirty
sock on the windowsill. We took photos of each other in
chalk-outline formation, pretending to be dead on the floor.
We slept with our passports in our underwear—a double
score for any would-be rapist! In a fit of hygiene control, I
turned my shirt inside out and used it as a pillowcase, sleeping on what looked like a dismembered pregnant lady. And
the next morning, in a spasm of realism regarding weeks of
dirty laundry, I put the shirt right back on. We couldn't let
the room win.

It didn't matter how many heroin addicts we found
slumped in the communal bathroom or prostitutes running
drunk through the halls. It didn't matter how many Gauloises
we had to smoke to mask the scent of armpits unwashed and
dreams deferred. We were going to love Paris. This trip was
our cultural vaccination. We'd see and do everything tour-
isty we could so that one day we might come back as real
adults and not have to go to a single museum or dead person's mansion. It was like tapas vacation. On day one, Emily

planned our first course: a whole day around cathedrals, culminating in her beloved Notre Dame. In pencil, she drew crosses on her map, most of which looked like X's. Which made the map as a whole look like that serial-killer-trailing one on police bulletin boards. I had moved past the Geneva train debacle and was happy to cede control in the matter of churches. Best, I thought, to get God out of the way as quickly as possible.

It's a strange concept, visiting a cathedral. A park is built expressly for visitors. So is a museum. Even the most avant-garde museums don't hang the art on the walls as it's being painted. But a cathedral has a whole other utilitarian life running parallel to the shrinelike patina of history. It's like visiting a work in progress. And the more elaborate the work, the more one feels as if one is intruding.

Emily's reaction to this was different from mine. Her experience seemed to be bolstered by the presence of real Parisians praying in pews. In one day, we had been to the Basilique du Sacré-Coeur, Saint Pierre de Montmartre, and the stained-glass light show that was Sainte Chapelle. By the time we hit Notre Dame, Emily had completely detached from the secular world in which she was raised. Maybe it was the buttresses. Maybe it was the tiers of votive candles or the embalmed saints. But my companion, a Protestant by birth, decided she wanted to confess.

"Noooo." I shook my head.

"Yessss." She nodded hers.

This seemed like too sudden a leap, just as all of Catholicism always seemed like too sudden a leap, regardless of the board from which one dove. Because we had a Christmas tree, I was never one of those Jewish kids who felt cheated out of the pageantry of an awesome winter holiday. There is a very specific frustration that accompanies an irreparably tangled string of lights, and I am familiar with it. But the downside to this candy-cane familiarity was a heightened curiosity about Christianity in general and Catholicism in specific. So one winter I asked my mother to explain to me the difference between most Christian denominations and Catholics. Which she obliged over cherry frosted Pop-Tarts.

"Protestants, for example," she said, cracking off a piece of Pop-Tart against a piece of Bounty, "believe that when they take the Eucharist, it's the symbol of the body of Christ."

I nodded. Symbolism was something I could get behind. The seder plate was an orgy of murderous analogies on a tray.

"Catholics, on the other hand, believe that they are literally taking in the blood and body of Christ."

"So, the cracker turns into Christ when they eat it?"

I imagined the safari-themed sponge capsules we used to get from the toy store. It's all neon-colored horse pills until you put them in the bathroom sink and boom: a hippo.

"Something like that," she agreed, putting the bloody toaster pastry between her lips.

Thus began my awe and fascination with the Catholics. The Catholics had magical powers. And damn it if they didn't know how to decorate. Christmas? Christmas was nothing. The first time I went to Easter services with a family friend, gilded eggs hung from the rafters. Women wore generously brimmed hats. They had the instincts to duck and weave the way civilians should but didn't with umbrellas. At the end of the sermon, an old man to my right said, "Peace be with you," and spontaneously hugged me.

"Oh," I whispered, and froze.

Eventually I gave in to this man's embrace, leaning into his musk. I had watched him brace against his walker and receive Communion, and now I was encircled by the arms of a person who had eaten Jesus.

There was something admirable about this way of thinking, something attractive about the sure leap into the invisible. An unadulterated bag of crazy? Yes. But admirable. No matter what your own beliefs may be, the mental fortitude required to think that *your* saliva has Rumpelstiltskinesque powers is something to be respected. Which is why I didn't want Emily fucking with it.

"I don't know if that's a good idea," I said, pointing at the palm of my hand and nodding toward a statue of the Virgin Mary.

Have you ever covered a flashlight with your fingers just

to watch your blood light up? That's how Emily looked at me—right through my skin and into my soul. Her eyes filled with hope.

In all likelihood, they were just irritated from the hotel sheets and watering because we misread the label on contact solution and bought mouthwash instead. But standing there in a cool stone corridor in Notre Dame, I knew we wouldn't be leaving unless she confessed. The power of Christ compelled her.

Of course, confessing in Notre Dame is not quite the same thing as confessing in your standard red velvet phone booth to the Almighty. This sin-purging line was fifteen people deep and at least half an hour long. And what it led to was not a curtain but a *très* large and *très* see-through glass office between two of the ancient pillars. From the outside, you could make out the backs of sinners' heads, bowing through a checklist of bad habits. It reminded me of the open cubicles of street-level bank branches in Manhattan, financial pet store windows. I am consistently impressed by their inhabitants' ability to keep their attention focused on their clients and their staplers so neatly aligned with their tape dispensers. Perhaps priests were able to do the same with God, lay him out on the desk and staple him into each wayward soul. Also like a bank branch, we lined up between slack velvet ropes. Up front was a paper sign slid into a metal frame. It read FRENCH/ENGLISH.

"Where do I start?" Emily was giddy with intimidation.

I hadn't thought of this—if you are nineteen and have never confessed, do you begin with the cigarette inhaled before noon this morning or the time you stole a package of sparkly pipe cleaners from your second-grade art class and kept them in the bottom of your closet for two years, eventually throwing them out because you felt so guilty? Do you mention the lying, the drinking, the cheating, the gambling, the masturbation, the schadenfreude, the disrespecting of your parents, the disrespecting of other people's parents, the doing of the drugs, the shoplifting of the gum, the coveting of worldly goods, the advantage-taking, the responsibility-foisting, the tone you use with food delivery people when you're alone and they're foreign, that time you had a hangnail on your toe so you stuck your foot in your mouth and you bit it off like a monkey? Or is that all kind of a given by now?

As we moved up the line, Emily kicking her giant backpack ahead of her, visitors solemnly but efficiently wove their way between the pews. They seemed disproportionately thrilled to be in a place that allowed flash photography. I feared for my friend's soul. If the End of Days came and it turns out the Catholics were right, would her soul come out like a deformed baby because she confessed only once? Was that not like getting half a piercing? We inched forward, ineffectively attempting to speed time by closing the space between us and the buxom Brit in front of us. She glared back at me, judge-y and annoyed. I took a step back and looked away. There was tourism and there was religion. Since when was it a good idea to cross the streams?

"Hey." Emily took me gently by the shoulder. "This is what churches are here for. To take people in and redeem them. It's on the Statue of Liberty."

"That doesn't make any sense."

"Yes, it does. The Statue of Liberty was a gift . . . from *France*."

It was Emily's turn. She stepped up, leaving me to fidget on the smooth stone floor. I looked around at the frozen pageantry of it all. My feet ached from traipsing from God's house to God's house all day. This man slept around more than George Washington. Similarly, one got the sense that God didn't actually *live* in all of these places. Sainte Chapelle was breathtaking, but Sainte Chapelle was a pied-à-terre. Notre Dame was home base.

"Are you waiting for your friend?" a man behind me asked in a heavy Italian accent. I was wearing very American shoes.

He was hoping I'd go sit in one of the pews. It wouldn't speed up his wait time, but at least it would provide the physical illusion. Which, it dawned on me, is all any of this was about, anyway. *Give me your tired, your poor, your Godless masses.* It was then that I made a decision that I'm sure had my grandmother rolling into the fetal position in her grave. I peeked through the glass to see Emily gesticulating wildly across from the priest.

"No, I'm actually waiting."

Ten minutes later, Emily opened the door. And the priest followed. *Oh, lord*, I thought. *What does one have to say to warrant being escorted out of confession? I told her not to mention the toe biting.* But while Emily met me in line, boasting the gratified look of the blessed, the priest put a new sign into the metal frame behind her. This one read FRENCH/JAPANESE.

Even God's servants need to change shifts.

A new priest appeared. Avoiding eye contact like a bartender on a Saturday night, he shut the glass door behind him and commenced readjusting the swivel chair behind the desk. I felt that internal conflict, that eternal struggle: Do I stay in this line now that I've waited this long or cut my losses and leave the building/movie theater/subway platform? I find it's better to stay and be frustrated than to leave and wonder.

I brushed past Emily and sat across from Priest 2.0. Deducing that I was not Japanese, he rattled off something priestly in French. I smiled at him. *Don't wink don't wink don't wink don't wink.*

"Je suis une Juden!" I blurted out.

This is what comes from seeing too many Holocaust films.

"But," I explained—my two favorite words in any foreign language are "but" and "because," the universal time-buyers—"but I think that it is true that we have the same God."

The priest put his elbows on the table and leaned forward, studying my face. Was this a prank? Why else would I willingly enter into a situation in which I couldn't function unless it was to mock God? I wanted to explain to him that I willingly enter into situations in which I can't function all the time, and it rarely has anything to do with God.

"English?"

"American!" I said, far too proudly. This was during a time when it was common to glue a Canadian flag patch on your backpack so that the natives would be thrown off your Yankee scent. Never mind the fact that anyone with a flag patch glued to their bag should probably have the crap beat out of them.

I had been in utero the last time this priest had uttered a coherent string of English, which he explained to me in words that were not only broken but utterly shattered. Like Helen-Keller-and-Jodie-Foster-in-*Nell*-had-a-love-child shattered. What a rare combination of languages lived in his godly head. What if it turns out that it's not an issue of beliefs but linguistics, and Saint Peter speaks only French and Japanese? Bummer.

The priest cleared his throat. We then proceeded to have the most awkward conversation of my life, potentially of his as well. Through the stilted silences, the rough combination of languages, and the pesky little fact that I did not believe in Jesus or wallpaper in kitchens came the following conclusions.

A. Paris was so beautiful because it made you look up at the sky/God.

B. If God had meant the French people to make sushi, he wouldn't have given them cows.

C. Little things in life can produce a smile on your face, like the pen he mindlessly clicked in his right hand, which he also let me click.

I could sense that our time was running out. I could also sense his feeling self-conscious about chucking me out, afraid I'd think it was because I was Jewish. He encouraged me to come back the next week when he was sure there would be an English-speaking priest manning God's fort.

"Ah, *oui*"—I looked at the clock—"but the week that is after this week I will not be here. I will be home."

At which point he got up from the desk and came over to my chair. I stood, and he took my hand.

"God is always home," he said, grinning.

I felt good, relieved, which is pretty much the equivalent of feeling good in organized religion. Relief. You're alive. God doesn't hate you. Your livestock is healthy. No one gave you boils today. Plus, the priest complimented my French.

"For how long have you it learned?"

The truth was, my French was atrocious for how long I it had learned. After a lifetime of flash cards and poetry recitation, I should have graduated from my *bicyclette rouge*

French. I should have been speaking sound-barrier-breaking Concord Rouge French. Out of my mouth came:

"Deux ans." Two years.

The priest looked at me long and hard.

"Vraiment? Deux ans?"

I gulped and pried my hand away from his. Yup. Uh-huh. Two years.

"Merveilleux."

"Oh . . . Mercy."

"You're welcome."

I flew out of the glass chamber and found Emily, who was standing beneath a large bloody cross. I pulled Emily's arm as if I were her toddler child and she wanted to go lingerie shopping. I had to get out of there immediately. I was a Jew, and I'd just lied to a priest in confession. In Notre Dame. I was going to get the shit smote out of me.

I had incurred God's permanent wrath and purchased myself a one-way ticket to hell. They only sell round-trips to zombies. At the very least, I was going wherever they send Jews who confess to priests and then lie to them. Oklahoma, maybe. But Emily was reluctant to leave. Apparently, her priest was multitalented. Not only was he a fluent English speaker but in her brief meeting with him, he had caused Emily to question her entire religious purpose on this earth, giving her a whole lot more to chew on than a wafer. She wanted to light candles and read pamphlets.

"Are you kidding me?" I said, eyeing the vaulted ceilings for signs of imminent collapse.

A security guard came over and tapped me on the shoulder. He asked me to keep it down.

"I'm sorry," I said, walking back toward the arches of sunlight coming from the main entrance. But when I turned around, I saw that Emily was still standing at the end of a pew. I whistled, the sound echoing in her direction.

Roused from her religious reverie, she picked up her giant backpack and made her way toward me. But not before one of her straps brushed against the table of prayer candles, knocking a corner one to the ground. Emily froze. The mess did not look dissimilar from, say, a jar of French mystery spread dropped out a window. I shut my eyes and exhaled. Surely, I thought, this happens all the time. Who puts a candle so close to the edge of a table? Who is so careless with other people's prayers?

The security guard glared at me. Between the two of us, I had been the first to get in trouble and was thus responsible for all subsequent offenses, even Emily's.

"I do not think you should come to this place again," he said, ushering us out with his eyes.

When we got outside, Emily unfolded her map, running her finger along the fold to find the next X. But I couldn't bring myself to go to another cathedral. We had seen the crown jewel. And I had gotten us escorted away from it.

Wasn't the whole idea of a tapas vacation to partake of a little of everything, anyway? I don't think God would want me to overdo it. I think he would want me to have a crêpe. So Emily and I compromised. No more cathedrals with low-lying fire, but we had to check *something* off the list. We went to the Luxembourg Gardens, where I stumbled upon my fountain. I stood in front of it while Emily checked out the sculpture garden, growing frustrated not with her map but with the actual sculptures if they weren't where they were meant to be. And because fountains are inanimate, and thus polylingual, I took the opportunity to use this particular fountain as my church. I apologized to God for everything I had ever done. Except for the stuff that was kind of a given.

THE RAIN HAD STOPPED, SO LOUISE SNAPPED THE umbrella shut. The fountain water was calm once more. Louise peered into it, her reflection blotched by the texture of the water. One woman's stagnant is another woman's still.

The remainder of our trip was spent in a less morbid fashion, imbibing the holy trinity of vacation beverages: coffee, wine, and liquor. For all its faults, tapas vacation had worked, and during round two, I felt no pressure to catalog every single Impressionist painter in one day. Instead, I discovered what I had slept through the first time: French nightlife. We accidentally found ourselves in a French strip club, where a Thai stripper named Cali kept touching Louise's hair. We went to bars, where I did the same thing in French as I do in English when people are shouting at me at close range but I still can't understand what they're saying. I shout back in extremely animated gibberish, which invariably results in much nodding and moving along of the conversation. Except I did this in an exaggerated French accent. It's better than the alternative—bellowing *"What?"* at thirty-second intervals, in which case everybody loses.

The last day of my visit, we went to a giant French flea market. I was determined to take a real piece of Paris back with me. For a long time, if people asked if they could bring me anything from their travels, I used to request a rock or a pebble. You shouldn't spend your time obligation shopping when you're on vacation. Plus, picking up a rock from the street was more legitimate than bringing back a snow globe not even manufactured in the corresponding country. I stopped making this request when a friend came back from South America and handed me a cloth sack with a rock— and a stowaway in the form of a dead insect serious enough to have an inch-thick exoskeleton.

At the flea market, I attempted to purchase a giant ostrich egg. I was bolstered by my ability to say *l'ouef* but ultimately thwarted by the *über mal* prospect of packing a forty-euro egg that was sure to break in my suitcase. In sixth grade, we conducted a science experiment in which all the students in the class had to drop an egg from the top of the school's building, protecting it from breaking using homemade devices. What brand of "science" this fell under, I couldn't say. Some kids cradled their egg in cotton-ball nests, some suspended it with rubber bands between sticks like a canopy bed. I squeezed an industrial-sized bottle of Palmolive into a large plastic bag, adding the egg halfway. Palmolive, as it turns out, is not as viscous as you'd think. Not only did the egg break but the bag exploded. It looked like someone had aborted a green chicken in the parking lot.

Louise and I were on our way out of the flea market, me resigned to allowing my *bicyclette rouge* French to deflate in the decade ahead, when I spotted a large antique wall thermometer. The dials were many and crafted; the glass was unbroken. How much could one, in good conscience, charge for a questionably functional wall thermometer? Five ostrich eggs' worth, apparently. It was a very nice-looking thermometer.

"Two hundred euro," the antiques dealer repeated as if it were a fact, a number measured using the object in question.

I bristled at the price, again employing *"mal,"* but this time it was exactly what I meant. After enough time in Paris my French had actually improved. But I was done talking. The first rule of any negotiation is be prepared to walk away. Or maybe that's the first rule of eating blowfish. Either way, it was a rule and it was out there and it was time to employ it. And then something happened. For the first time since Paris and I had gotten to know each other, one of its citizens asked me to return.

"One hundred seventy-five euro," said the antiques dealer.

Actually, he didn't say this, he wrote it down, employing the long French *1*. My French had gotten better but not that better. Large numbers were on the same ring of vocabulary as nutritional information. Once he gave in a little, it was all the bolstering I needed to negotiate down, until it was only two ostrich eggs' worth. There is a bittersweet capitalist tingle when one gets too good a bargain. The glee of separating yourself from the idiot who pays full price is quickly replaced by the fact that someone was trying to rip you off in the first place. Everyone's the idiot eventually.

On the crowded metro back to the center of town, I attempted to protect the thermometer. It was wrapped in layers of newspaper and bubble wrap, but I was dubious about its prospects for staying in one piece. I didn't even have any dish soap.

"*S'il vous plaît,*" I'd say when jostled, melodramatically cradling the thermometer. "*C'est un violon.*"

Louise whipped around to look at me.

"*Ceci n'est pas un violon,* " she whisper-shouted.

"Shut it, Magritte. It is now."

Though "thermometer" surely falls under the ten-letter translation rule, I have no idea how to say "valuable antique wall *thermomèteuuur*" in French. Even if I did, I assume the average person's ability to conjure an image of such a thing is on par with my ability to produce the words to describe it. Plus, there are benefits to lying about such things. If you are over the age of ten and in possession of a classical musical instrument, people think you are a genius. They think you have an innate gift that you have harnessed into a tangible life skill. They look admiringly at your hands.

Back in the sublet, the thermometer leaned a good foot beyond my suitcase despite my generous angling of it. *This is not a problem!* said my laid-back self, recalling the time it had run through the Miami airport with two carry-ons and an oversized lamp made out of a lawn flamingo and still made the flight.

Shut up and eat your Ding Dongs, I thought, and left the room.

My flight was the first one out of Paris. Louise and I stayed up all night, eating cheese and drinking the last of the wine. I left for the airport while it was still dark outside, making sure to leave time to call a taxi and then for the taxi not to come. I hailed a cab on the street and loaded my suitcase in the trunk but held the thermometer close to my chest. The streets of Paris were utterly abandoned as the taxi darted through them. I lowered my window to take in my last moments of Parisian air. Then I put it back up as we drove past a garbage dump and a gas station.

I tore open the bubble wrap on the thermometer. I just wanted to touch it. Finally, something pertaining to Paris had worked out in my favor. Back when his ostrich-egg count was still at four, the antiques dealer said he purchased the thermometer at an estate sale. I imagined the original owners and hoped that they would not be too upset to see it go home with an American. I felt a seam of some sort on the back of it. Curious, I tore a little further to feel a sliding brass hook. I looked up at the cabdriver through the rearview mirror. I put the thermometer on my lap and pushed the hook, opening the back panel like a grandfather clock. I thought I might find a treasure map. *The Goonies* was a movie, sure, but a very realistic one. Or perhaps I'd discover a copy of the French Declaration of Independence. Certainly not *our* Declaration of Independence. Copies of *that* thing turn up only behind maps of West Virginia and velvet Elvis paintings. We are the least classy treasure hunters on the planet.

TREASURE HUNTER'S ASSISTANT: *Do you think the scroll is beneath the seventeenth-century farmhouse? Or maybe in this dusty urn I just found? Looks like it's from Greece.*

Treasure Hunter in Charge: *Nahh. Crack open that keepsake ornament with the glitter bonnet. I'm pretty sure it's in there.*

My thermometer was scroll-free. However, if there was ever any doubt about the thermometer being from the 1800s, I had my answer: in lieu of pendulums and chimes, it was filled with vials of mercury. Not just a bead or two, as in twentieth-century thermometers, but a post-apocalyptic supply dangling from chain after chain. For a moment I entertained the idea that the silver was on the outside of the glass, painted on there for some olden-timey reason I couldn't fathom but which would make perfect sense if explained to me on a guided tour of Versailles. *As you can see here, folks, the toilets were sealed shut with beeswax each night. Can anyone tell me why? That's right, to ward off pig ghosts . . .*

Maybe the vials themselves were empty. But when I turned them upside down, the mercury did what mercury does—holds on for a heartbeat, fighting gravity like ice at the end of a glass before it comes crashing down on your teeth.

"Fuck."

"*Pardon?*" My cabdriver looked at me through the mirror.

"Rien." I sighed, reattaching the tape. *Okay, this is a bit of a problem!*

Having just checked the airline's website for the most current regulations regarding hair conditioner, I knew that mercury was not among the substances welcomed by the TSA. I think it's generally important—nay, American—to know why you're being told a rule exists. Which is why I went online to begin with. But if it's four a.m. and you're full of French wine, there's really nothing funnier than the TSA website. There is no personality type untouched, no scenario unexplored, no rare-weapons collector unaddressed. The more obscure the warning, the better. I like to think I would be seated next to the guy who pitched a fit because he didn't realize he had to check his throwing stars and "realistic replicas of explosives." He'd probably gnaw his plastic water cup into a shiv out of resentment. It was in the midst of all this that I learned that, in addition to causing lockjawed flipper babies, mercury will eat through aluminum. Which is what planes are made of.

So it's not actually the explosiveness of mercury that's a problem, no more than the handle of the knife or the center of the throwing star is a problem. You have to be a pretty genius terrorist to know how to make a bomb out of mercury. But you have to be only an average idiot to poke a hole in the plane.

My plan was, for once, to stay very still and do nothing. In stressful situations, people often talk about a fight-or-flight response. Which, in my option, doesn't give enough credit to the more common reaction of curling up into a little ball. My history of explaining myself in Paris was peppered with failure. For once, I made the decision to play it cool. Or stupid. Whichever came first.

The good news is that I arrived at the airport with plenty of time to be detained by security. Apparently, grinning like a moron as you slide sketchily wrapped prohibited substances through an X-ray machine will not make it okay that you have them on your person. I attempted to buddy up to the security personnel by getting them on my team, being overly cooperative as they escorted me into a small glass-paneled room noticeably reminiscent of the confession booth in Notre Dame. This was not the first time I had been taken to the special "threat to society" security room at the airport. The first time was when I had booked a sudden and nonsensical jaunt to Portugal and back. But at least in that instance, I possessed the confidence of innocence.

Three guards, two women and a man with boobs, put on latex gloves, and one of them handed me a pair of scissors so that I might autopsy the mysterious package myself. For no particular reason beyond being given a knifelike object, I imagined stabbing one of them with the closed scissors. An excessive means of teaching them the hypocrisies of airport security? Sure, but in the visual, I also knew karate. So I hoped it wouldn't come to that.

Two of the guards stood behind me as I sliced open the

top of the bubble wrap. I thought this would be satisfactory. You could see the wooden top of something decorative. No wires or egg timers here. Still, they encouraged me to keep cutting. As I roughly sliced through layers of tape and plastic, I thought, *If I was going to blow up a plane, why would I do it so conspicuously?* Terrorism isn't customarily the terrain of reverse psychology. *Ceci n'est pas un ticking suitcase!* The whole Trojan horse bit doesn't have a place in the era of metal detectors.

No matter, I still retained a skeptical appreciation for the law. Sometimes the best way to see your tax dollars at work and protectors in action is to get caught yourself. It's when they gestured for me to take off my shirt that I lost that.

"Pardon?"

"Your shirt," said one of the female guards, pointing to make herself clear.

In my carelessness with the scissors, I had actually managed to cut my shirt along with the bubble wrap. *Surely,* I thought, *this will get me off the hook. I can't even cut bubble wrap successfully. Who's going to blow up a plane? Not I.*

She picked up the thermometer and held it the way one might hold a rabbit one has just shot. She quickly felt along the body for any irregularities but found none. She set it down and they all ran cotton swabs over the thermometer and consulted their military-style computer. They took turns frowning at one another, then at the thermometer, and then at the hole in my shirt. Something was showing up on the screen, but they couldn't categorize it. Whatever traditional bombs are made out of, this was not it. There must be some rarely registered airport security category that also includes gunpowder. If you are guilty of possession of these rudimentary explosives, men in wigs and brass-buttoned coats take you into yet another room and slap you senseless with their gloves. Only then may you board the plane.

Man Boobs called in a supervisor, a diminutive but determined gentleman with bags under his eyes that looked like mine but permanent. He asked me to have a seat. He wanted to know where I got the thermometer, and I told him. He wanted to know when I had purchased it, and I told him. He wanted to know if I had purchased it or if someone had purchased it for me, and I told him, adding an "I wish." He wanted to know how much I had paid for it, and I beamed when I told him. But I wasn't about to tell them about the mercury. I had made it this far. The thermometer was the one piece of Paris that was mine. I was a terrible godless lying American idiot, but the fucking thermometer was mine.

Bracing for the possibility of a lie-detector test, I tried to wind my mind back like a speedometer. Only a few hours earlier I was still ignorant of the thermometer's innards. I looked at the digital clock on the desk. I could feel myself about to confess. All I wanted was to crack open a fleece blanket as the flight attendants encouraged me to peruse my options for duty-free grilling equipment and Clinique.

"Okay." The supervisor clicked his pen and slid it into his shirt pocket. "Just make sure you declare it at customs when you land."

You mean if I land, I thought. If I really did have designs on blowing up the plane between here and New York, notifying customs was a bit of a moot point. It made me wonder what else they were willing to let go. I yanked my shirt down so that the hole was more of a slit and less of a belly-button peep show. I put the thermometer underneath my arm like the musical instrument it wasn't. A woman's voice came through the PA system, first in French and then in English. My plane was starting to board. I got up and thanked them for detaining me.

Off the Back of a Truck

f you have to ask, you can't afford it. This is the second most useful piece of romantic advice I have ever received. It arrived at our house with the Tiffany catalog, that manual so thick it had to be forcibly removed from the mailbox. Unlike other catalogs, with their cheap vertebrae of staples down their spines, this one was fused with glue. There were no prices listed in it. It was just layout after layout devoted to isolated jewels, as if they were criminals. Their crime? Fostering unreasonable desires in the hearts of consumers. There were moonstone necklaces that would pay for college. Not like tuition. Like to found a college. There were earrings that would rip the lobes off your face and call you Sally for crying about it. There was an amethyst bow that froze, sorority sweet, for the camera but smuggled a sharp weapon behind its back. The catalog opened with antique estate jewelry. This was the Blinging Out the

Dead section—one-of-a-kind baubles older than sea turtles. They dared you to imagine all they had seen. And you accepted, leaning into the gloss of the page until you could almost make out your own reflection. Had they been loved? Ignored? Better traveled than you'd ever be? These sparkly roaches would outlive everyone. This ring, that necklace, had been with a person, now gone, on the best day of her life and the worst. And so they were reminders of how very odd it is to be young. When you are ten or eleven, you know in your heart that you have yet to hit either of those days. But both are out there. Waiting for you. One like the shiny front of a brooch and one like the piercing tack hinged to the back.

In the latter half of the catalog were the engagement rings so new they held the promise of a whole life yet to come. But a very specific kind of life. Here, said the book, here is what your epilepsy-inducing diamond will look like from above. Here is the angle at which you will show it off to your friends. Here is what it will look like tilted and sliding with sweat as you shake hands with a squash racquet even though you don't even like squash. Harold likes squash. And you don't see why you have to like everything a man twenty years your senior likes. Now here is the ring digging into your hand with each unforced error, pressing the very spot where your fifth-grade boyfriend once placed a ring made of gum wrappers. Finally, here is what your ring will look like in profile when you remove it in a Ritz-Carlton in Dallas four years hence, placing it on the nightstand along with a stranger's watch and what's left of your blackened heart.

I preferred the honest morbidity of the estate section.

I showed my mother a ruby necklace and opened my mouth to ask the obvious question.

"If you have to ask, you can't afford it."

"Okay, but let's guess how much it's worth anyway."

I flipped the catalog back toward me. I was just home from school and swiveling on a kitchen stool while she breaded things.

"Our dining room table and chairs?" I offered. "Grandma's dining room table? That thing's oak."

It wasn't only that we couldn't afford this jewelry, it was that I had never met anyone who could. It was like the jewelry of Narnia. Maybe there was an index of prices in the back. Even criminals had to hold up a little sign with numbers on it.

"Let's not and say we did," said my mother, invoking my sister's favorite conversation ender. "Set the table."

"It's set."

"I don't see napkins," she said, not turning around. She put her hand over an open jar of olives and flipped it over the sink. "And I don't want to have this discussion with you."

My parents, as a rule, refused to talk about money. Even if it was fake money. So I began bidding on the jewelry, using kitchen supplies. Did we think an emerald necklace was worth the same as eighty mustard jars and one hundred boxes of frozen spätzle? Have you ever had frozen spätzle? It's amazing.

"Maybe if this was the end of the world and people lived off mustard. But the thing is," she said, olive juice streaming through her fingers as she doled out her first most useful piece of advice, "you should never wear anything you can't afford to lose."

AND THEN I PROMPTLY FORGOT THE ENTIRE CONversation for fifteen years. Partially because at the time we were talking inanimate objects, not boys, and partially because these nuggets of wisdom were an eyesore of practicality in the midst of an exceedingly impractical time. Coveting was commonplace. Kids were being mugged for Air Jordans and leather eight-ball jackets. So, sure, from a strictly life-or-death standpoint, you shouldn't wear something that will get you shot. Or even slapped around a bit. No one can afford to sacrifice their life defending a piece of mass-produced rubber. But that's not advice, that's Darwinism.

As an adult, of course, the symbolism of these twin philosophies is as apparent as a punch to the face with a fistful of diamonds. If you have to ask someone to change, to tell you they love you, to bring wine to dinner, to call you when they land, you can't afford to be with them. It's not worth the price, even though, just like the Tiffany catalog, no one tells you what that price is. You set it yourself, and if you're lucky it's reasonable. You have a sense of when you're about to go bankrupt. Your own sense of self-worth takes the wheel and says, *Enough of this shit. Stop making excuses. No one's that busy at work. No one's allergic to whipped cream. There are too cell phones in Sweden.* But most people don't get lucky. They get human. They get crushes. This means you irrationally mortgage what little logic you own to pay for this one thing. This relationship is an impulse buy, and you'll figure out if it's worth it later.

So, assuming you've gone ahead and purposefully ignored the first adage because it doesn't apply to you and you are in love the way no one in the history of spooning has ever been in love: now what? You've gotten what you want, but the state of mutual ownership has shifted. Like that piece of jewelry that you're never quite comfortable wearing, you become concerned with its whereabouts, who borrows it and for how long. You wonder if you'll lose it, if it might look better wrapped around someone else's neck. Admit it: wouldn't it be less stressful not having it touching your body at all?

WHAT DID STAY WITH ME FROM THE DAY THE TIFfany catalog landed was a fascination with and proclivity toward material impracticality. For example, I had some idealistic fantasies about my first studio apartment. I was going to build a sliding bookshelf ladder, install a chandelier, purchase an old subway turnstile from a scrap yard and put it in just inside the door. Slutty, yes, but not as slutty if I could find one that didn't require tokens. The ceilings in my studio kitchen were pointlessly high, and at least once I thought, *I could keep a midget up there. I could build a cubby and rent it out to a midget.* I would bake in the winter to keep him warm, maybe toss him balls of raw cookie dough. In reality I was trolling stoop sales for shelving units, figuring out how I was going to pay an entire electric bill on my own. And yet a week after I had signed my lease, I found myself walking into the most overpriced furniture store on Fifth Avenue. Just because it was there and I was there. It wasn't going to kill anything but time for me to look. Just to look. Pawning a napkin ring from this place would solve the electric bill conundrum.

The store took up three floors and was called something like Out of Your League or I Sleep in What You're Wearing. Nothing within its walls ever went on sale. (A policy that must be a source of comfort for its regular customers, who will never have that "God damn it" moment six months after their purchase.) Every item speaks the same rarified language so that what you're really paying for isn't an object but fluency in the dialogue of wealth.

The more daunting pieces of furniture lived on the top

floor, where a loft space was split into fake living rooms. And if nothing else, I was in the market to be daunted. The elevator itself was meticulously designed, down to the hand-stitched upholstered bench on which I sat. It's extremely rare to be alone in Midtown Manhattan outside of a post-apocalyptic film. Instead of the silence-inducing panic and an acute curiosity about the edibility of dog meat, it lends itself to everyone's favorite game: *What If This Was My House?* Often played at art galleries and upstairs bars, it also works for more unexpected spaces. Like botanical gardens. I know this fern terrarium is humid, but will you look at that light? Will you? *Look at it.* The third floor got a whole lot of light.

In the corner was a giant wheel of hanging carpets, hand-woven into thick geometric shapes that flapped down, form-ing the world's fanciest car wash. They were the kind of rugs that would look great beneath a full-sized crystal chan-delier. The kind of rug you look at and think, *I could really see my midget lounging on this.* But like an oversized spinning display of personalized key chains, I did not expect to find one that called my name. Or my wallet. Which is when I saw it. Not too big, not too small, striped in all the right places. I pushed the other rugs away to get a better view and stroked it with my palm. How much could an area rug possibly cost? Even one spun from goat chin hair and fairy semen. *Let's guess how much it's worth, anyway.*

Four thousand dollars. Not including tax.

"Holy shit," I yelped, unhanding the carpet as if it had burned me.

"Can I help you?"

A burly man in a pit-stained T-shirt emerged from a stockroom door. A door that blended into the wall, as the ones in the Oval Office do. He did not look like he was part of the Out of Your League corporate family. Or, rather, he looked like he could have worked in a different Out of Your League chain. Like a Home Depot. Or a steak house. Anywhere I felt equally out of my depth.

"Noooo." I stepped backward. "I don't think so."

"It's not cheap," he said, gesturing around at the porcelain birdhouses and hand-painted garden fences. "But maybe I can help you with something on another floor?"

I declined and made my way back to the elevator. Suddenly I felt self-conscious. I didn't mind this man thinking I had enough money to be in the store. I minded him thinking I spent it on porcelain birdhouses.

"I don't suppose the rugs ever go on sale?" I asked the already answered question and pressed the already lit button.

"Nah." He paused for a moment. "But give me your number, and I'll call you if they do."

The elevator came, a gaping little gullet that would carry me back to street level, where I belonged. I looked at him, watched him lightly wheeze. I let the elevator door shut.

"I'm Daryl." He shook my hand.

"Daryl, if the carpets never go on sale, why would there be a reason to call?"

"Well, sometimes they have display discounts in case the stuff gets beat up being in the store. From foot traffic."

We looked around simultaneously at the gleaming wooden floors, our joint focus settling on the rack of carpets that were not, in fact, touching the floor. I smelled pine.

"So you have sample sales?"

"What's a sample sale?"

"Blink once if the carpets go on sale, twice for no sale."

He winked at me. This was an unproductive conversation. But he insisted on exchanging numbers. I thought, *Fine, give Daryl the three-hundred-pound handyman who probably doesn't work here but killed five old ladies in the stockroom your number. Who's it going to hurt?* I scribbled it on a piece of scrap paper, along with my name, watching him as I wrote. His face remained stoic as he handed me his self-printed card. I had made it no more than three blocks when my cell phone rang, a foreign configuration of numbers on the display.

"Hey, Solange."

"I think you have the wrong number."

"It's Daryl. From five minutes ago."

"Oh. Hey."

"I found you that carpet."

"That was quick." I stopped short on the street.

"I looked in the system, and the Greenwich company store has a display carpet. It's the one you were looking at."

"That's funny." I held a finger against my free ear. "I didn't know you guys had a company store in Greenwich."

Daryl proceeded to describe a fairly simple process by which I would meet him at a street corner of my choosing away from the store. I would give him three hundred fifty dollars in cash. In return, I would receive a packing slip with a routing number. Because this was about the shadiest thing I'd ever heard, I felt compelled to tell Daryl, "That's about the shadiest thing I've ever heard."

And because I wanted the carpet, I made plans to meet him during my lunch break the next day. I told myself that this was an overpriced item. I was basically getting it whole-sale. It was the same as if I was an employee of the company. Clearly the universe was trying to give me a housewarming present. I wasn't about to tell the universe to go fuck itself by rejecting its bountiful bounty. Plus, if I paid less for it I could afford to destroy it. It was only a carpet, not an eight-ball jacket. More than anything, it just didn't feel like steal-ing. Which, I am aware, is a paltry excuse for a crime. Ladies and gentlemen of the jury, it just didn't *feel* like murder. Oh, well, okay, be on your way, then.

IN THE MEANTIME, I HAD TO GET DOWNTOWN. I WAS meeting a gentleman named Ben. I had only ever really seen Ben in passing at book parties. But the Venn diagram of people we knew in common had become so saturated, it seemed that our not knowing each other was the one space to be filled in. We were growing tired of friends insisting that we knew each other when we didn't, grabbing our arms and explaining that we must be mistaken. As if the harder they squeezed, the more likely they'd get an *Oh, BEN. You mean roommate Ben. Kidney donor Ben. Siamese twin Ben. Sorry, took me a minute.*

I knew I was in trouble the minute I opened the door. He sat at the end of the bar performing a series of unremarkable actions: reading a magazine, chatting with the bartender, unsticking a cocktail napkin from the bottom of a whiskey glass. If I may confirm your suspicions: things will not end pleasantly with this person. I understand that this is the point at which I'm meant to provide some salient physical details particular to Ben and Ben alone. That way, when this situation turns sour, it's clear I had something to cry over. But perhaps we can strike some sort of deal in which you pretend I have told you all the things you need to hear so that you might sufficiently mourn along with me. Because it's not for lack of desire that I withhold these finer points. It's that sometimes I think I will never be able to conjure his face again. I can get the eyes and the mouth if I try, but the nose could be anyone's nose. Same with the forehead. Kind of blurred into deformity. The mind is like any other organ—it will be kind and healthy to you if you are kind and healthy to it—so when I consciously stopped thinking about Ben, my mind took over the heavy lifting for me. *Are you ready to go back to* Titanic? Sure, fine, what the hell. Bring me a glass of something and roll the footage. I am ready. But not able. My Ben memories have fallen victim to a kind of Russian-nesting-doll effect in which a person becomes smaller and more poorly rendered with each layer. The more buried the romance, the less surface area there is to work with. The strokes become sloppy.

Plus, as it is with every set of nesting dolls, no matter how many or how few, there is always that one at the center that won't open.

"What are you reading?" I picked up his magazine.

"It's not *The Atlantic Monthly*," said face-blurred Ben.

I held it up and flipped to the cover.

"Yes, it is."

"It's a ploy to get me out of talking to the bartender about the medical coverage for his prostate surgery."

I looked over to see the bartender examining the mirror behind the liquor bottles, picking something out of his teeth with one of those drink stirrers they put holes in to trick you into thinking they're straws. He looked over at us and waved with the stirrer, a little pole with no flag.

"You'd think just the surgery would be sufficiently inappropriate." I nodded back at the bartender.

"Turns out"—Ben shook his head—"he used to *work* for *The Atlantic Monthly*."

"Ahh, that *is* unfortunate. You should've gone with *Cat Fancy*."

"Well, now I don't need it." He tucked the magazine into his back pocket. "Now I have you."

I was hoping to skip a process I had seen too many coworkers go through. All arts industries are abnormally incestuous, and book publishing is no exception. Not only do you have the quantity of time spent working together but the quality of spare-time interests. Which can make going to work as painful as an exposed nerve if you don't like the people you work with. These people are not just asking you to attend meetings, they're *infringing on your mind*. Although some demands on your time can make you see soul mates in your coworkers if you do like them. These are your desert-island people. You got into this game not because you were particularly skilled at the same things but because you liked the same things. You spend every meal with them. You call one another at night and swap work dreams in the morning. *How do we first begin to covet, Clarice?*

Imagine the degree of romantic delusion festering in these artfully dressed youths, thinking they have finally found their tribe . . . well. People are bound to get naked eventually.

Of course, down the road, everyone revolts. They want off the island. They'll happily sleep with anyone who has never heard of their latest packaged cultural progeny, who becomes conscious of a new artist for the first time when they read about him in a magazine. How refreshing! An engineer, a teacher, a doctor. Bring it! A chef, a banker, a pencil maker. No, scratch the pencil maker. Too close to home. But now what? Now the real danger begins. We grow frustrated with these down-to-earth partners and their irksome normality. We seek the ease of shorthand and grieve for the comfort of synchronized priorities—a relationship in which no one will ever say to the other, "What are you so stressed about? It's not world hunger." In a cycle that's not vicious but stale, we return to what we know best, shutting ourselves off for good and never leaving our immediate radius again. It's like *No Exit* with a better soundtrack and a kick-ass library.

"I'm sorry I'm late." I dragged out a stool. And here I lied: the eyes I can remember. A dirty peridot color. Gleaming with the devil's presence. Or perhaps contacts.

"Here." He reached for my bag with one hand and felt for hooks beneath the bar with the other.

As we talked, I realized there was one other tiny little hiccup. Ben had a girlfriend. I couldn't remember how I knew this, but know it I did. He had not informed me of said girlfriend, not mentioned her once, but it was one of those relationships with a duration that qualifies for common-law marriage. They owned parakeets. They had seen each other's passport photos. They split the electric bill. These facts seeped into my mind through tribal osmosis. I thought perhaps I was making the tension up, anyway. I was superimposing my attraction, creeping out into the road and painting an extra lane for traffic to flow in the opposite direction. But four rounds later, I had entered a bad country song. Literally. It was the jukebox's genre of choice. We drank whiskey through mixer sticks until we were the only ones there. Ben touched my knee and left his hand there, ready to blame the carelessness of his extremities on alcohol. I didn't move it. Eventually, I excused myself to go to the bathroom. I leaned on the sink, looked seriously at the mirror, and slapped myself in the face.

Dolly Parton's "Stay Out of My Bedroom" was playing outside. I thought, as many have thought before me: what would Dolly do? I once saw an interview with Dolly in which she described being a young girl, biting her lips and pinching her cheeks before dates because she wasn't allowed to use makeup. There was only one thing to do. I slapped the other side of my face to even things out.

"Should we go?"

While I was bursting blood vessels in the toilet, the bartender had placed the stools on top of tables in an inhospitable position.

"I guess we should," Ben said, looking at me without blinking.

"Awesome." I took out my wallet. In the course of my opening it and his insisting I shut it, Daryl's card came tumbling out onto the bar.

"You dropped this." He unfolded it. "Should I be jealous?"

"Oh, God." I snatched it back. "I need that in case he doesn't show."

"In case who doesn't show?"

I told him about Daryl and the rug and the pit stains. I told him about my new apartment, which would lead to my new life and how we are drawn to things we can't afford and people call it "taste" to make it palatable but what it really is is a kind of superficial cloying for happiness. But I was young and in my prime cloying years, so this was okay. And instead of telling me it was morally wrong and moderately illegal, he kissed me.

THE NEXT DAY, FRESH FROM THE ATM, I WAITED on a bustling Midtown street corner near my office. Daryl pulled up in a black Kia with gleaming rims and rolled down a magenta-tinted window. People stared. I leaned in, trying to push the actual documentary *Pimps Up, Hos Down: Hookers at the Point* to the further recesses of my mind. I made small talk about where he had come from, the fact that he owned a car. I couldn't tell where the parameters of the conversation should be, and was impressed by all cars. Even ones with naked-lady air-fresheners hanging from the rearview mirror. *How humiliating for her,* I thought. To be stripped naked, back arched, and for what? Her home *still* stank of feet and cologne. I reached over through the passenger window and flicked her, sending her spinning.

Daryl handed me a sticker with a bar code on it.

"There could be a bunch of bananas headed my way, couldn't there? Please don't send me three hundred fifty dollars' worth of bananas. Or any bananas at all."

I couldn't let go of the envelope of cash. The magenta tint was peeling from the edge of the window like skin.

"Well, Solange." Daryl slung his forearm over the steering wheel. "Life is like a box of chocolates."

"Sloane . . ." I mumbled. "And I know. You never know what you're gonna get."

"No, man. Shit's picked over, and it makes your ass fat."

"That's pretty funny," I said as I released the money.

Apparently, you don't need a gun to rob me. Just get me into a dark alley and tell me a decent joke.

Two days later a giant padded roll appeared outside my front door. Another tenant must have dragged it in. It leaned against my door frame, where it slumped, imposing but lazy, like an off-duty guard. I kicked it into my apartment. When I cut the strings to unfurl it, the carpet revealed what I already knew in my heart to be true. The fresh-off-the-loom scent wafted through the air. I checked the packing label to confirm it had been shipped not from an outlet in Greenwich but directly from the company's factory in Queens. This was a brand-new carpet. You could eat off it. Though you wouldn't dare.

"Yo. Solange. Did you get the carpet?"

Ever the service-oriented thief, Daryl called to check on his delivery. I would soon learn that calls from Daryl originated from a different number every time, a habit that seemed spylike in theory but massively inconvenient in reality. Who keeps so many phones? Who borrows so many? And why? His identity-masking also had the inverse effect, though I didn't have the heart to tell him. Daryl— along with my parents, who still block their home number for privacy—was my perpetual Unknown Number. Like blank tiles in Scrabble. Yes, they can be any letter you wish, but in the end there are only two tiles. It's the telecommunication equivalent of pissing in a pool that turns your urine blue.

"Yes, Daryl." I sat in the middle of my mat of shame. "It's in great shape for a sample."

Daryl knew that I knew that he knew that I knew that this thing had come off the back of a truck. But I wanted it out there, on the record for both of us, that I was not consciously participating in the black-market transfer of luxury home furnishings. Let the record show that while I may not have been innocent, I spoke the speech of an innocent person.

"Well"—he smirked through the phone—"there's not a lot of foot traffic in the store where it came from."

Apparently, he wanted the same thing. And apparently, carpets were not the only "display" items available courtesy of Daryl's warehouse on wheels. Why, just in were a shipment of hand-blown drawer pulls that may or may not have been damaged in transit. Was I interested? Reader, I was. Daryl and I had wisely thrown ourselves into the deep end with the carpet transaction. If the retail value of such a big-ticket item had made it past my thin moral filter, I had no business flinching at some lousy drawer pulls. It was a gateway carpet. So we agreed to meet in Union Square, where I would again come bearing a wad of cash, though slightly less thick than last time. In return, Daryl would send me a package of possibly chipped cabinet handles and drawer pulls from the outlet in Greenwich.

My money was on unchipped.

BEN HAD CALLED EVERY DAY FOR FOUR DAYS, HIS messages packed with charming jokes about the anthropomorphic nature of his relationship with my voice mail. I programmed his name into my phone without a last name. My phone-programming policy runs backward: if I barely know you, you go by your first name, and preferably an abbreviated version of that. Once we've been trapped in a bomb shelter together, forced to repopulate the human race as we know it, you get a last name. On the fifth day, I picked up.

"I thought you had a girlfriend."

"I would like to see you again."

"I'm sensing that. But you know," I whispered hostilely, "if I were a girl and called some guy every day for four days, I would be having what we like to refer to as 'a psychotic break.'"

"You are a girl."

"I'm trying to point out a double standard here."

"But when I do it?"

I didn't know what to say. Rather, I knew what to say, and it wasn't English. Whatever sound a cell phone snapping shut makes was the only appropriate one.

"Meet me in Union Square after work," he said, tentatively authoritative. "We'll get coffee. If it makes you feel better, I'll let you pay."

"I do have to be there this afternoon, anyway."

We sat on a park bench, Ben and I, with a metal armrest strategically between us. It was the start of fall, that time of year when everyone walks around New York declaring how hot it is for this time of year. It hasn't been *cold* cold in September in twenty years, and yet every year we are shocked. The emergence of roasted-nut vendors on the sidewalk and colored leaves in the elementary school windows won't stop you from sweating. Unless you put more thought into it than is normal, you end up wearing outfits that do not say "fashionable" so much as they say "uncle." And so I sat in my temporally schizophrenic linen dress and tall leather boots. I shoved the dress material under my knees to keep the wind away as Ben explained that tribal osmosis never lies.

He did, in fact, have a long-term girlfriend. Until recently. They were broken up. The pain was fresh. It was raw. It was grade D but edible. Her name was Lauren, and she designed retro underwear. He had moved out of their apartment, granting her sole custody of the birds and the phone bill, and was subletting a place nearby. Actually, he could point to his new bedroom window from where we sat, and did so. Something about seeing the window turned me puritanical. Probably because I knew how inevitable it was that I would soon see this bench from the other side. I looked at the ground.

Ben and this woman had been dating for longer than I'd owned anything I was wearing, including my breasts. I had questions. Questions delivered to my brain in bunches, tied with ribbons of anxiety. Where were his things? Who broke up with whom? Were they on speaking terms? If she was his in-case-of-emergency person and he was hit by a bus but lived, they'd probably get back together, right? The worst terrorist attack in American history was recent enough, and it had taught us that disasters make you appreciate what you already have, not what you barely know. But I felt I couldn't afford to gamble on the answers. The truth was,

I was elated by this information. I adored this information in all its validating glory. But I also worried about the fragility of it. *Purty rabbit. Crack! Dead.* And so I asked nothing. Ben leaned over the cold armrest and held my hand. I pulled it back.

"I have a meeting." I got up, glancing at the rubber band around my wrist where a watch might go.

"After what I just told you? Are you serious?"

"Yes. As a heart attack."

"Can you maybe pick something equally serious but less medical?"

"As an eight-year relationship?"

Really, I just didn't want him laying eyes on Daryl. How would I explain the suspect majesty that was Daryl? Clearly the idea of him, the card with his phone number, held its appeal. But the real-life physicality of Daryl had a darkness to it, a seedy underbelly that was more like an all-over-belly. Daryl in person was not my edgy connection to low-grade illegal activity but an inmate-looking person, stuffed into his clothes like they were sausage skin. No one likes to see how the sausage gets made. So I leaned down and kissed Ben and told him to call me. I'd even pick up this time.

I remember the salty-sweet combination of excitement and relief we both felt. Excitement at the start of a new love affair and relief that we had found each other despite the anti-incestuousness policy we had. Beyond that was the special relief we both reserved for him: he had narrowly escaped a scrape in which he would be with the wrong woman for the rest of his life. Like the man said the night we met: *Now I have you.* I actually preferred it when all of this was unspoken. It was when he spoke of it, outlined his feelings with such intensity and detail, that I should have been more concerned. But how can you be concerned with those eyes? How can you be concerned when a man who lives clear across town is waiting on your stoop as you leave for work in the morning, surprising you with coffee? When you describe a movie you saw when you were so little you think maybe you dreamed it and so he tracks down a copy of it? How can you be concerned when you see that twinkle in his family's and friends' eyes that says, *Thank God, you are nothing like her?* Or when you come out of the bathroom on a Sunday morning, looking like you've been hit by the night-life truck, and he says, "I wake up every morning wanting to see you"? Then he shakes his head at the girlishness of his own confession and invites you to some family event many months from now.

These incidents are not cause for concern. They are cause to program his last name into your phone.

SOME PEOPLE HAVE COKE GUYS. I HAD AN UPHOL-stery guy. As the months rolled by, my acquisitions from Daryl could be parsed into two major categories. The first was home goods. Dishes, trivets, a lamp, a doorknob, and a throw pillow you'd sooner shield from an atomic bomb than throw anywhere. All well out of my price range and all packed like cattle into my new studio. I was a fence. A really, really nicely decorated fence. With only the faintest twinges of guilt, I accepted compliments from friends on my new goods. My mother came to visit and commented on how savvy I was, stretching my publishing-house salary to support these furnishings. The nicer my belongings became, the more the savvy transferred back her way, a personal compliment to her frugal-purchase-imbuing parenting skills. This is the good thing about furniture. As opposed to precious jewelry, no one is ever quite sure how much it costs. No one will believe you found an emerald ring in a nest of diamonds in a cereal box, but there are people in this world lucky enough to find original Eames chairs at flea markets. I just wasn't one of them.

The second category was information about Daryl himself. I learned a lot about what made Daryl Daryl, most of which I am no better for knowing. He hated in general and liked in specific. He hated most music. He hated the homeless. He hated desktop computers. He hated subway lines that never went aboveground. He hated pygmies, and when I asked him to provide me with an example of pygmy exposure, he described, in detail, the Puerto Rican Day Parade. He liked certain strip clubs and certain strippers on a pole-to-pole basis. He loved his car. He thought tropical places were overrated, except for South Beach in Miami, because the one time he went there it was quiet and there weren't any homeless people. When I told him this was not the standard impression of South Beach, he told me that everyone I knew was going to the wrong part. He liked chicken sandwiches and bought them constantly, despite being critical of their mayo-to-meat ratio.

"Why don't you just make your own chicken sandwiches and bring them in to work? Sometimes I make my lunch."

"I can't." Daryl rubbed his belly, leaning on a traffic light on the corner of Twenty-third and Park. "Because then I'll have all this chicken lying around the house and I'll eat it before it gets to the sandwich."

"I have that problem, too."

"And I'm not allowed to eat in the stockroom."

"Oh, okay." I laughed, and took my most recent packing slip.

Siphoning off thousands of dollars of merchandise from the company was one thing, but a Subway sandwich wrapper in the trash can? The man had his limits.

ONE NIGHT I WAS COMING HOME LATE, TREATING myself to a post-midnight cab tour of the city, when I realized I had developed Ben's tic of wanting to see him all day. And by "tic" I mean complete infatuation. We were, in a word, disgusting. Slightly inebriated, I reached for my phone. Finding lip balm instead, I applied it, distracted like an animal. What was I looking for again? Oh, yes. I held the phone close to my face. Nothing goes together quite so well as drunk people and buttons. I left what my drunken self was sure was an adorably articulate message. Which is when Ben's voice mail came to life, calling me from the other line.

"How dare you," I hiccupped. "Your voice mail was about to say something brilliant."

Silence.

"Hello?"

The phone went dead.

It had been just under a year since I'd met Ben in the bar. Just when I was becoming entirely relaxed in my relationship (as a show of good affection, I had put Ben's middle name in my phone), he started behaving oddly. I couldn't put my finger on it, but while I wasn't looking we had thinned from two very busy people to one very busy person.

The faucet of affection had slowed to a drip. One morning I got up early and went downtown. I waited on his stoop with coffee. He kissed me on the cheek. Was this how relationships worked? One person always at the foot of the stairs and one at the top? That actually seemed pretty accurate for most couples I knew, but surely it did not apply to us. Soon I became hyper-aware of when I had called him last. I began fishing for compliments, picking fights, inciting jealousy whenever possible through a variety of pulse-checking activities that registered on the same scale as a lightbulb going out. You just think, *Oh, that happened,* and screw in another one. While Ben was in the bathroom, I flipped over a postcard on his refrigerator and found myself at once comforted and disappointed to see the "Love, Mom" at the border. When he returned from a trip and called me, I heard a noise and asked him if he was at baggage claim.

"No." He seemed perfectly bored by the question. "That's the TV."

"Oh, so you're home already?"

I had an antique hair clip that I used very judiciously. The clasp was on its last screw. Given its advancing age, I knew I was allotted a limited number of uses when I bought it. Ben loved to play with it every time he came to my apartment, pressing it open as if it were a mechanical pen. Click, click, click. This thing I had opened and shut no more than a dozen times. Click, click, click. I could feel one eye narrowing as though afflicted with a cartoon migraine. Every word out of his mouth was eclipsed by the sound of metal breaking away from tortoiseshell.

"Could you stop that, please?"

"Stop what?" *Click.*

I couldn't take it anymore. I leaped off the bed, ready to grab it from his hand.

"That."

One thing that's embarrassing is standing naked in front of someone, having transformed from a sex object into a scolding maternal figure. Or the reverse, a little girl who puts such proprietary stock in meaningless things. It's especially awkward if this comes at a point when you have morphed into every bad cliché about your own gender, like some mutant multiwinged butterfly come out of the crazy cocoon that looked so smooth from the outside.

"I think someone's being a li-ttle paranoid," he said, and clicked it one more time.

It broke into pieces.

I held still, waiting for things to go back to the way they were. This behavior, right now, was the abnormality. It reminded me of when I was in elementary school and had a textbook with a drawing of a woman in it. Some kids looked at the picture and saw an old witch and some saw a young girl. Whatever you saw you could unsee if someone showed you how. Change the nose to an elbow, a neck to a skirt, a wart to an eye. See her now? I always saw the witch first. I'd try to surprise myself, sneak up on the book with the young girl in mind, open my eyes and . . . Nope. Witch.

"It doesn't matter," said my teacher. "The point of the exercise is to see what you want to see."

"But what if I don't *want* to see the witch?"

It's not the worst thing in the world to choose to believe the bad is temporary and the good is permanent. It's just not the smartest.

Lauren! It had to be Lauren. He needed closure, not

coffee. I suggested they have lunch together. At this point, I was friends with all my exes. Not in a forced "Collect all five!" kind of way, but in that way you make nice with everyone in your early twenties. When it seems impossible that a deep connection with another person could just go away instead of changing form. It seems impossible that you will one day look up and say the words "I used to date someone who lived in that building," referring to a three-year relationship. As simple as if it was a pizza place that is now a dry cleaner's. It happens. Keep walking.

As soon as it left my mouth, I realized that it wasn't my place to suggest. I would have to be dating Ben for years before I lapped Lauren in the area of personal wisdom.

"I don't think that's a great idea," Ben confirmed my intern status.

My plan negged, I felt oddly like the child of Ben and this woman I had never met. Up until this point, I had thought we could all be like a Woody Allen film. We could be great friends, and our humor would stem from the fact that there was no way in hell we should get along this well. In addition to an emotional suspension of disbelief, that would require us all being equals. Suddenly, I was the Soon-Yi. I did not want to be the Soon-Yi. I also didn't want to be the Mia, the one who finds the Polaroids. It was bad enough I was turning over the postcards. Woody was the only pure option, and that role had already been cast.

———————

BEN WAS OUT OF TOWN AND I WAS IN THE MIDDLE of a work dinner, seated at a packed table covered in baskets of calamari and advance copies of books, when my phone rang. People around me held conversations on the diagonal. I fumbled in my bag underneath the bench and grabbed it. Unknown Number.

"Hello?" I shouted. "Daryl?"

"Doug?" the voice said. "Is this Doug?"

"I'm sorry, I think you have the wrong number."

For Christ's sake, was there no one in this town who could get my name right?

"Sloane?"

"This is she."

"It's Lauren. Ben's girlfriend."

You know that sensation when you lift up a carton of milk you expect to find full but it's empty, and it goes flying through the air with surprising force?

"Could you hold on for just one second?"

I slid roughly over the knees of people next to me and went outside. By now there was no confusion about the weather. It was *cold* cold. I held my jacket closed with my fist.

"Hi," she said.

"Hi. Not to be rude, but how did you get my phone number?"

"It was in Ben's phone."

"Not to be dense, but how did you get Ben's phone?"

"He went out to pick up food and I took it off his desk."

And there was Ben's face, stuck to the side of the milk carton, missing. I sat on the curb as the bombs went off: Lauren and Ben had never broken up. True, they were having problems grave enough to warrant an auxiliary housing situation, but every absence from our relationship could be explained by his attendance in theirs. Unlike her underwear line, their relationship wasn't retro. It was happening in the present tense. She asked me where I was on his birthday, and when I said it had not come yet, she said, "Yes, it has." I asked where she thought he was going all those mornings when he appeared on my stoop.

"He told me he was going to work out."

"Maybe he was," I suggested. "Maybe he ran to my place."

While I had been belatedly paranoid and prematurely blind, Lauren had been on the case for months. I imagined her like a lawyer with a highlighter and a Visa bill as she rattled off Ben's crimes, a parakeet perched on her shoulder. The parakeet is wearing an eye patch, though I can't say why. He repeats the word "bastard" a lot.

Her reason for calling, I had to understand, lay in her loyalty to other women. It wasn't to confront me. Though she was sure yelling a lot for a nonconfrontational person.

The trash talk swirled around, cycling up like a tornado until it was just a wind of generalizations about herself and the power of her relationship with Ben. I immediately questioned the strength of a relationship in which one party waits for the other party to get Chinese food and scrolls through his or her cell phone, hunting for mistress aliases. Instead, I let her wrap up a tirade that was mostly rhetorical, including questions like "How can I respect myself if I can't respect myself respecting him?" and "I mean, Scorpios, right?"

The party inside was filing out, off to their respective homes or second evenings. Someone handed me my bag, which I accepted in a zombie-like trance. Despite the cliché generalizations about female empowerment only a women who designed lingerie could produce, I liked Lauren. Maybe I wanted to keep her on the phone because I felt outside myself, and from this third-party perspective, well—this whole thing was pretty juicy. Talking to her was like talking to the part of Ben I had been missing but unable to identify. Mostly I think it was because we both loved the same thing. And we had both paid too much for it.

"I don't like to press the fates, mind you," she said.

"Of course." I nodded.

"But I tried to call you once. He had you in his phone under Doug. Then I wasn't sure it was you, so I hung up."

"Really?" My voice cracked. "Just 'Doug'?"

———

I GUESS YOU COULD SAY I WAS HURT. THAT WOULD be fair. When Ben returned home, dumplings in hand, Lauren confronted him. Dim and then some, he denied the whole thing. Ben and I had met once, perhaps twice. Just the two of us? No, never by ourselves. When? Oh, who can remember these things when all other women meld into one giant asexual boob? Denial in the age of e-mail. Gutsy. When Lauren explained that she had spoken to me directly, Ben explained back that I had constructed the entire rela-tionship out of whiskey and psychosis and glue. I know all this because Lauren called me the next morning to tell me about it.

"Why do you still have his phone?"

I was lying on my beautiful carpet and looking up at my pointlessly high ceiling, still wearing the same outfit I had worn the previous night. I was compiling a list in my head titled *Reasons to Get Up*: *You Don't Have to Leave, but You Can't Pee Here.*

"I turned it off and hid it in my underwear drawer," Lau-ren said proudly.

"That would be the first place I'd look for it if I were dating you."

"I also hid his contact lenses."

I wiped mascara-laced chunks of sleep from my eye.

"What I don't understand is why he didn't just use my

real name. Why have a stranger's name under a pseudonym? Aren't I strange enough already?"

This didn't scratch the surface of what I didn't understand. The fake name seemed the least essential detail on which to focus, a two-second lie at the end of a yearlong relationship. It was like nailing Al Capone on tax fraud. But the bigger picture was too difficult to understand. In that picture, the person I loved not only stepped out of the frame but turned around on his way out to tell me he was never there.

"He said he could barely picture your face."

My heart shuffled past my spine, out my back, and melted into the carpet.

"I guess he can't be expected to picture much if you hid his contacts. I have to go now."

I hung up the phone. For days it rang with his number. I could never be sure who was on the other end, so I just watched it go, watched it become silent after each ring. Then, like the movie villain who seems dead but comes back to life to grab the closest ankle, the message beep would jar me afresh. The messages were long and mostly from Ben, who had clearly located his phone. It occurred to me that if Lauren was the kind of girlfriend who knew to check her boyfriend's address book and Ben was the kind of boyfriend who knew where to find stolen items, maybe they really were destined to be together. The messages vacillated between begging and chastising, between affection and reprimand, often in the course of one monologue. Then they got tired of chasing their own tails and just stopped.

I couldn't cry. Within a week, I had transitioned to a kind of purgahurt where the idea of being mollified by pints of ice cream and the idea of stabbing myself in the chest seemed equally unviable. And yet the world seemed hell-bent on handing me daggers. Every cab ride home managed to swing me past his sublet apartment, which was apparently his actual apartment, or his office building. Who was he, the Church? NYU? It seemed greedy for one individual to have so much landmark property. I'd look out the opposite window, longing for a time in the near future when it wouldn't occur to me to look or not look. Every restaurant suggested was one I had been to with Ben. Horribly insensitive friends marked their own birthdays with celebrations, re-signed leases in his neighborhood, used words with vowels he also used. Unsolicited advice came pouring in, each serving as lovingly doled and useless as the next. I'd nod and agree to make it stop. *You're so right, they do call it a cliché for a reason.* All the while reminding myself to keep a list of people to punch in the face when I had opinions about things again. *Plenty of fish!* said the friends. True. But why is it that when you don't need them, all the fish are in a barrel, waiting to be shot, and when you'd like them around, they're all in the sea?

The worst, because it is always the worst, was the music. Maybe Daryl was right when he eschewed it altogether. "I" is the loneliest vowel that you'll ever do. At first, most songs I heard became poignant. This included ones that were in no way from a woman's perspective or even the jilted party's perspective. I was a good girl—but I did not love horses or Jesus and I'd burn America to the ground in exchange for a sliver of my former happiness. But surely this is what Ben felt: free. Then songs with no conventional poignancy whatsoever became poignant. It takes a level of creative depression to hear "Girls Just Wanna Have Fun" and weep. After a while, my masochism grew impatient, deviating from the path of daily activity to seek out voluntary torture fixes. I bought Dolly Parton's greatest hits. I'd wake up before dawn with the lyrics of Carly Simon's version of "In the Wee Small Hours" running through my head and lazily out of my mouth. It was like the worst poetry slam you've never been to. When I fell back asleep, my subconscious was lazy and repetitive: There was the dream in which we attend a kid's pool party and he lets me drown. Then there was the other one in which I am trailing him in a rental car and lose him, a flash of Lauren's arm dangling a bra from the passenger-seat window.

Almost everyone has the identical response to such behavior: *That sucks. How long were you dating?*

This is, without exception, the first thing people want to know. I can never figure out what they're really asking. Do they want to know if you have a right to your reaction? Are you to be dusted off and sent to play or rushed to the emergency room? How stupid are you, exactly? They hang on to the math. Math, friend to so few in this life, is now like a shipment of cheese fries at fat camp. Math will save you. Math—proportional, statistical, syllogistical—has your back. Simply fork over the answer to one harmless little question and math will show you the end of the road.

There's one formula for two months and another for five years. Suddenly everyone's a break-up numerologist who will stop at nothing to convince you of their infallible relationship with time and space. It takes half the duration of the entire relationship to get the other party out of your system. Sex with strangers can speed the process if it's the right stranger, delay it if it's the wrong one. There are rules for that, too. You listen intently to your friends. You marvel at what an exhausting enterprise this is, quantifying grief. You let them purchase alcohol for you. This will work out nicely for everyone. They get to believe you are absorbing valuable wisdom, and you? You get drunk. After drinks, they go home to their girlfriends and boyfriends, who ask: *How is she? Not so good*, they respond. *Well*—the girlfriends and boyfriends shrug—*how long were they dating again?*

Meanwhile, in a bed built for one across town, you look meaningfully at your ceiling, believing you have glimpsed into the heart of *The Matrix*. What is *wrong* with these people? How can they be so cold?

Nothing. Nothing is wrong with them. You must not blame them for believing that heartbreak is one size fits all, more like a shoelace and less like a perfume. They, too, have been heartbroken. Their pain was no less than yours. In some cases, it was worse. There *is* a pecking order to pain. Deference is due to those who have recently gone through a divorce. If there are children involved, their parents win. Coming in behind them are those who purchased property or own a business together. Deep down, you are grateful for these people. They are generous with their own lives, happy to turn themselves into cautionary tales, starting each conversation with "It could have been worse." Unfortunately, because you are actually out of your mind, you think, *It was worse.*

One friend tells you a story of breaking his ankle running through the steep hills of San Francisco in his boxers at five a.m. on the way to bang on the door of a girl who broke his heart. And who wasn't home, anyway, because she was sleeping with his best friend. What you take away from this is: don't get broken up with in San Francisco. But what he is *trying* to say is that the math has done wonders for him. Time has passed, and he tells the story as if it didn't even happen to him. The fact of it makes him laugh. Laugh!

"What are you going to do?" he says. "You have to move on. You deserve better."

You are encouraged to focus on the other person's flaws, which, come on, shouldn't present much of a challenge in your case. You say you feel stupid. You say that you loved him, as if this will win whatever argument you're having with yourself. Your friend puts his arm around you and says that part of growing up is realizing that love is a lot of things, but it isn't everything. People bring their own stories and their own issues to the table.

"It has nothing to do with you," he says.

By now four months have gone by. You get asked if you still miss him. Don't answer that. At this point in your life, you are about as stable as a table made even by sugar packets. Anything you say comes from the same self-involved brain that only weeks ago brought you such gems as "Is there is a difference between wanting to be unconscious and not caring if you're unconscious?" In your spare time—and let's face it, all of it is spare—you have been quietly ticking off private holidays and "this time last year" anniversaries. If you want out of this conversation, you're going to have to cough up the big lie.

You miss the *idea* of him.

There you go. Was that so hard?

"That goes away, too," says your friend.

Through the magic of the biological imperative, his brain has been reprogrammed. He has been forced to gloss over his own romantic carnage so that he might once again start down that road of procreation. He has nineteen layers of skin; you have three-fourths of a layer.

They're all like this, the recovered. Sometimes you want to hop across the table, curl up in their laps, and beg to be made one of them. How does it work? Hypnosis? A chip in the neck? A radioactive spider with Xanax venom? Your brain is oatmeal, and they can separate it for you. They can wield their sanity like a metal spoon because they have what you don't: math. They can predict the exact day you will congratulate yourself for not thinking about him. That day is a placeholder for the real day, which will follow about a month later. This is the day when you actually won't think about him. Your very happiness, you see, depends on how long. How long? How long? Say it fast enough and it sounds like the name of a dead emperor. Ho-Lung of the Sad Sap dynasty.

My whole life, okay? You have been silent for months, and more than anything, this is what you want to say: *We were dating my whole life. And I don't mean symbolically, as in I keep going for the same type of guy and this is a pattern that needs exploring. Like paisley. I mean, I was born and he was born and then we fell in love. And now all I have is a memory that won't quit and some choice words for Carly Simon.*

Instead, you just round up by a month and leave it at that.

I BOUGHT MYSELF A JUICER. THE EXCURSION TO BUY the juicer was something to do on a weekend morning. It made me feel good to fake human interaction, to ask the salesperson questions. I liked the weight of the plastic bag, and I liked taking it out of the box and throwing away the instructions. I bought a sack of oranges, carrying them with the confidence of someone who is happy and healthy. I was going to juice the living shit out of these oranges.

My mistake, after a year of spending too much on things and people I couldn't afford, had been in purchasing the second-cheapest juicer available. This was a counter space–friendly device equipped with the same handle used to roll down the windows in a Ford pinto. And with about the same end result. The juicer was far more interested in splitting the skin of the fruit than it was in procuring juice from it. I assaulted orange after orange, squeezing the lever harder each time. The only noticeable result of my brute force was the seeds that appeared in the juice.

Finally, I shoved the juicer aside. I sat on my kitchen floor with a salad bowl and a pile of orange halves in my lap. I dug my fingers into them, squeezing the fruit against the skin, crushing them with my bare hands, frustrated and crying. I was never going to fall in love again. I was going to die alone, surrounded by juicers and bread makers and a hundred other DIY gadgets meant for people who have too much time on their hands and never have sex. I cried the dry, openmouthed kind and then the dripping kind and then the kind where you can't breathe. Which is when the phone rang. I sprang to my sticky feet, grabbing it like a track-and-field baton.

"Yo. Solange."

"Oh. Hey, Daryl," I said, detaching wisps of hair from the citrus-salt mixture that coated my face.

"How'd you know it's me?"

"Because, Daryl, that's not my name, and you're the only person who calls me that."

"Oh. I'm sorry. You want a tuffet?"

"What's a tuffet?"

"You know, like Little Miss Muffet."

"Oh, right." I sniffed.

"You okay?"

"I'm fine."

"You don't sound fine. You been crying?"

"Where do you want me to meet you?"

"Is this about a man?"

"That's a big word for what he is."

I told Daryl that this was the last time. One tuffet and I was out. I knew what I needed, and it wasn't math. I needed this year to be over. I needed to start rounding my time with Ben down instead of up. I needed the anniversaries to run their course. And Daryl was a part of this year. In recent nights I had been breaking a cardinal break-up rule by fantasizing about the interior of Ben's apartment. I'd try to think sexual thoughts that didn't involve him. When that proved difficult, I tried to find loopholes. Like replacing him with his friends. But why did his friends persist in taking me back to his apartment all the time? Where was their loyalty? So I'd move the whole show over to my place. But the friends got lost in the transfer, and when I shut my eyes, all I saw was Ben, lounging on my bed or my carpet. Annoyed, I'd try to remove every piece of furniture I owned, hoping his ghost would be sitting on the sofa when it left. But things always snapped straight back to the way they were. It was too hard to imagine my apartment unfurnished anymore. It was filled with such beautiful things.

THE NURSERY RHYME ENDS WHEN A SPIDER COMES along and frightens Miss Muffet straight off her tuffet. I have wondered about what kind of lesson this is for a young girl. If you're eating your curds and whey and a spider comes along, I don't think there's anything wrong with picking up a newspaper, smashing it, and going back to your breakfast. Perhaps if the rhyme was illustrated not with a young girl in pigtails but with the image before me—that of Daryl on West Eleventh Street, sitting on a pastel tuffet—it would end differently.

"What the hell, Daryl?" I said, coming down the street toward the West Side Highway.

His thighs spilled over the sides of the tuffet so that it looked less like he was sitting on a cushion and more like he was shitting ottoman legs. He wobbled up into a standing position. This was going to be less portable than a packing slip.

"It's a sample from the store."

I rolled my eyes. "Yeah, I know. They're all 'samples.'"

"No." He easily lifted the tuffet in the air to show me the scratch marks on the bottom. "For real."

I rubbed my fingertips against the worn base and touched the cushion. If it could remain fluffed with a bunch of rich ladies and then Daryl sitting on it, it was probably worth having. He offered to help me load it into a cab if I wanted. Then he asked me if I wanted to talk about it.

"About what?"

"You look skinny," he said, still holding the tuffet against his chest like a teddy bear.

He didn't mean it as a compliment. I cocked my head at him. Daryl's beard was growing in everywhere except over a white scar and some pockmarks on his chin. His nose, perhaps once in proportion to his face, had become oddly narrow in adulthood, and he sniffed a lot. His forehead had one big wrinkle across it that touched down on both temples like a fleshy rainbow. I can still picture that face perfectly.

"Pull up a chair, Daryl," I said.

He placed the tuffet gingerly on the pavement. I looked around me. I had not yet run into Ben. I couldn't shake the feeling that such a run-in and requisite awkwardness were inescapable. The same love affair runoff that had melted New York into a quaint town had become worrisome once I stepped back over the line. Or, rather, once I was pushed. Ben could be anywhere. He could be sitting on the next crowded subway car I squished my way into. And I would have to stand there, my crotch in his face, his face in a folded magazine, his magazine still warm from his back pocket. Though he never was on the subway cars. Or the street corners. Or anywhere else outside the confines of my brain. I longed for invisibility but was sincerely shocked when I got it.

Daryl tugged at his pants until he could sit comfortably in them. I told him everything, starting with the moment I slid the stool away from the bar, and when I was through, he said, "That's some Jerry Springer shit right there."

"There wasn't any pulling of the hair or applying of Vaseline to the face."

"Some Ricki Lake shit, then."

"I'll give you that. But people are fucked up, Daryl. They bring their own stories and their own issues to the table. Part of growing up is realizing that love isn't everything."

"You don't actually believe that, do you?"

"You know." I smiled and gave up. "I don't."

"Good." Daryl seemed satisfied that I had not crossed over into the bitter and black-hearted. "So now I'll tell you what no one else will."

For all the many bits of trivia I knew about Daryl, I did not know if he was in a relationship. I knew nothing of his track record with women, only that they probably weren't homeless pygmy computer owners. Besides, I already knew what no one else would tell me. I had known it forever. You shouldn't wear anything you can't afford to lose. Which is exactly what I did when I put all my eggs in Ben's bottom-less basket. I had the citrus carnage to prove it, dried and rotting in my kitchen trash. Daryl looked up at me from his cushion, a sidewalk Buddha.

"What won't people tell me?" I asked him, bracing myself for another cliché about chocolates or fish.

"It wasn't as real as you thought it was. Whatever anyone else tells you is bullshit."

Then he slung the tuffet under his arm in headlock position and we waited in silence on the corner until a cab came. He closed the door slowly behind me, making sure it didn't smash the delicate and already-scuffed legs of the tuffet. What a tragedy it would be to drag it all the way out here for nothing.

TIME PASSED, AND I FOUND MYSELF WANDERING into Out of Your League—where I was apparently wearing an outfit that indicated I should be followed around like a fourteen-year-old shoplifter. I took the elevator up to the third floor. The inlaid pine still reflected the lights of the chandeliers above it. The layout was the same, but a few new items had come in, including a line of bath products. Just in case you wanted to smell as expensive as your oven mitts. I went over to the carpet wheel and spun, but I couldn't find one to fall in love with. I think I had just outgrown my fascination with the store in general. A thin, older saleslady in pearls lowered her glasses and asked me if she could help me with anything. But I could tell she didn't mean it.

"I think I'm set." I waved, repeatedly pressing the button for the ground floor while she pretended not to judge me.

What can you do? Time grabs you by the scruff of your neck and drags you forward. You get over it, of course. Everyone was right about that. One mathematically insignificant day, you stop hoping for happiness and become actually happy. Okay, on occasion, you do worry about yourself. You worry about what this experience has tapped into. What will be left of it when the surface area shrinks? How will you make sense of it after the compulsion to have others make sense of it for you has faded? There is one thing you know for sure, one fact that never fails to comfort you: the worst day of your life wasn't in there, in that mess. And it will do you good to remember the best day of your life wasn't in there, either. But another person brought you closer to those borders than you had been, and maybe that's not such a bad thing. Knowing what you can afford is useful information, even if you don't want it. It dawns on you that this is what's in that last nesting doll that won't open. Somewhere in the center of all that bargaining and investing and stealing is meaning and truth and the lessons you have always known. You hope so. Because without meaning, it was all just a bunch of somebody else's stuff.

ACKNOWLEDGMENTS

It's pretty awkward when you write a normal-size book but have a lot of people to thank. It says everything good about the generosity of the thankees and nothing good about my ability to dress and feed myself. So here's to the people without whom I would be less of everything:

At Riverhead: Sean McDonald and Emily Bell (patron saints of Preventing Me from Looking Stupid), Geoff Kloske, Kate Stark, Michael Barson, and Katie Grinch. It is a privilege to be published by people who laugh at the same things.

At WME: Jay Mandel (a living retort to the "No one will care about your baby as much as you do" adage), Lauren Heller Whitney, Erin Malone, and Jake Sugarman.

At Vintage: Russell Perreault, Jennifer Jackson, Lisa Weinert, Anne Messitte, Sonny Mehta, Chip Kidd, and every editor, publicist, and author who has looked up from their own manuscripts to ask, "How is yours coming?"

At home: Luc Sante's *Low Life* was invaluable when learning about the door policies of nineteenth-century brothels. Also helpful but not as good a read: *In Flight Portuguese*.

At 3 a.m.: Dana Naberezny, Elizabeth Spiers, Kate Lee, Paula Froelich, Josh Kendall, Ethan Rutherford, Kimberly Burns, Sean Howe, Chris Wilson, Chris Tennant, Mickey Rapkin, Boris Kachka, Leigh Belz, Eric Lovecchio, Elizabeth Currid, Megan O'Rourke (for the sharp eye), Nick Stern (for the title), Heather Gould, and Angela Petrella (for the permanent loans), and L.D. (for wherever you are).

Thank you.

Also available from *New York Times* bestselling author

SLOANE CROSLEY

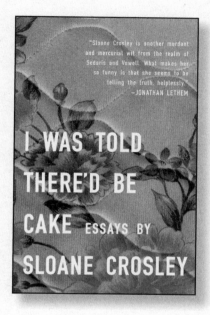

"The essays in this exquisite collection, Crosley's first, spin around a young woman's growing up and her first experiences in a big city, New York, as it happens. The voice feels a little like Nora Ephron's, a little like Dorothy Parker's and David Sedaris's, although Crosley has a spry wistfulness that's very much her own...[T]he arrival of a very funny writer." —*Los Angeles Times*

AVAILABLE NOW FROM RIVERHEAD BOOKS

sloanecrosley.com
riverheadbooks.com

T129.1010